D-Day to Carpiquet

The North Shore Regiment and the Liberation of Europe

D1453277

The New Brunswick Military Heritage Series, Volume 9

D-Day to Carpiquet

THE NORTH SHORE REGIMENT AND THE LIBERATION OF EUROPE

Marc Milner

**GOOSE LANE EDITIONS and
THE NEW BRUNSWICK MILITARY HERITAGE PROJECT**

Edited by Brent Wilson.
Front cover: *Battle for Carpiquet Airport* (detail) by O.N. Fisher, CWM 197 10261-6183.
Back cover: *Smashed German Beach Anti-Tank Gun, Normandy 4 July 1944* by O.N. Fisher, CWM 197 1026-6375.
Cover and interior page design by Julie Scriver.
Printed in Canada.
10 9 8 7 6 5 4 3

Library and Archives Canada Cataloguing in Publication
Milner, Marc
    D-Day to Carpiquet: the North Shore Regiment and the liberation
of Europe / Marc Milner.

(New Brunswick military heritage series; 9)
Co-published by New Brunswick Military History Project.
Includes bibliographical references and index.
ISBN 978-0-86492-489-6

1. Canada. Canadian Army. Battalion, New Brunswick Regiment (North Shore), 1st — History.
2. World War, 1939-1945 — Regimental histories — Canada.
3. World War, 1939-1945 — Campaigns — France — Normandy.
4. World War, 1939-1945 — Campaigns — France — Carpiquet.
5. Carpiquet (France) — History, Military.
I. New Brunswick Military Heritage Project II. Title. III. Series.
D756.5.N6M495 2007   940.54'2142   C2007-900462-8

Goose Lane Editions acknowledges the financial support of the Canada Council for the Arts, the government of Canada through the Canada Book Fund (CBF), and the government of New Brunswick through the Department of Wellness, Culture and Sport.

Goose Lane Editions
Suite 330, 500 Beaverbrook Court
Fredericton, New Brunswick
CANADA E3B 5X4
www.gooselane.com

New Brunswick Military Heritage Project
The Brigadier Milton F. Gregg, VC,
Centre for the Study of War and Society
University of New Brunswick
PO Box 4400
Fredericton, New Brunswick
Canada E3B 5A3
www.unb.ca/nbmhp

MIX
Paper from
responsible sources
FSC
www.fsc.org   FSC® C011825

To Gunner W.C. "Bill" Milner, 13 RCA
who fought alongside the North Shore Regiment
throughout the campaign and admired their courage

Iconic footage of the D-Day landings: the North Shore Regiment comes ashore on A Company's beach at la Rive Plage, just before 0800 June 6, 1944. <small>Canadian Forces Film Unit</small>

A portion of the film footage appears as kinescopic images towards the bottom of the right-hand pages throughout the book. The film can be "played" by fanning the pages from front to back.

Contents

Members of A Company pose near Anguerny, June 8, 1944. Front row:
Syd Cable, Frank Cripps, and Vince Nolan. Back row: "Red" Cripps, Bill
Clancy, and Marven Harding. LAC

Introduction

In the early hours of July 4, 1944, the 1st Battalion The North Shore (New Brunswick) Regiment (NSR) deployed into a grain field two and a half kilometres west of the French village of Carpiquet. Most of the men had stormed the Normandy beaches a month earlier, and they had spent the intervening weeks holding the line. By July, they were battle--hardened veterans. But nothing in their experience had prepared them for Carpiquet. As the NSR waited for its attack to commence, many had premonitions of death. One group of six men from the Acadian Peninsula had talked through the night, wondering aloud who among them would survive the coming battle. Three did not. Only Omer Larocque from Lamèque Island remained on his feet the next day — and he had shrapnel in his leg. Other survivors told similar stories.

When the barrage started at 0500 hours, the battalion, with le Régiment de la Chaudière to their right, moved forward into a maelstrom that poured down on them from three sides. Only the dust and smoke from the relentless explosions offered any cov-er during that tortuous crossing of the open grain field. The two-and-a-half-kilometre plunge into the German line by the NSR and other battalions of the 8th Canadian Infantry Brigade was like poking a stick into a wasp's nest. Throughout the fourth, the bombar-

ment of Carpiquet village was remorseless: the Germans claimed there would be no one left to stop their counterattacks. They were wrong. On the first night in Carpiquet, the NSR and its supporting forces stopped five attacks launched by the elite of the German army. Unable to dislodge the Canadians, and with their own casualties mounting, the Germans brought down a rain of fire on the village that did not abate until the nearby city of Caen was liberated on July 10.

The NSR endured Carpiquet with stoicism and courage, and at great cost. "I saw reinforcements come up to us in the evening," Padre Myles Hickey wrote after the war, "and I would bury them the following morning." By the time the battle was over, 370 Canadians had been killed or wounded, 270 of them from the NSR. These losses gutted the fighting strength of the North Shore's rifle companies, and their replacements — drawn from across Canada — permanently altered the composition of the battalion. Small wonder that the "hell called Carpiquet" was remembered by North Shore veterans as the graveyard of the regiment.

Few people know the story of the North Shore Regiment and its remarkable accomplishments in the liberation of Europe during the Second World War. Drawn from a rural part of a very rural province, the NSR had no stellar lineage or great social cachet. Its ranks were filled with farmers, fishermen, woodsworkers, and mill hands, drawn largely from tough Scots, Irish, and Acadian settlers along the Baie des Chaleurs, the Acadian Peninsula, and the Miramichi River. Its non-commissioned officers (NCOs) — the sergeants and corporals — were typically shop foremen or gang bosses, ordinary guys with little formal education. The NSR officers were drawn largely from the social elites of society, men with money and status, although by 1944 some were from humble backgrounds who had climbed the ranks of the pre-war militia. With few exceptions the bulk of the battalion came from isolated family farms, tiny fishing villages, Native reserves, and small urban centres like Dalhousie and Newcastle. They shared many things in common, including a rough pride in eking a living from the land and sea in the tough climate of northern New Brunswick. Most exhibited a self-reliance borne of necessity, were comfortable in the woods with a rifle, understood field-craft instinctively, were inured to hardship and privation, and expected to move from job to job without much reward or recognition. Fishing, hunting, baseball, and hockey were their passions, and most were Roman Catholics. All that said, they had their differences. About twenty percent were Acadians, many of whom spoke no English when they joined, and the divide between the Miramichi and the communities along the Chaleurs and between urban and rural was often pronounced. At least twice during their long years of training in England, NSR commanding officers took advantage of changes in battalion organization to shuffle their troops around, breaking up cliques and welding the unit together.

By the time the NSR landed on the beaches of Normandy, it was reckoned to be one of the top two battalions in the Canadian Army. That's probably why it got the nod to land in the initial assault, the only regiment from a rural area in the leading wave on the Canadian beaches. It also had, arguably, the toughest task of any Canadian battalion landing on D-Day. Certainly it was the only one tasked with both breaching the beach defences and then tackling a series of heavily fortified positions laid out in depth behind the seafront. In the event, the NSR failed to achieve all its D-Day objectives, a failure mitigated by the fact that it took a whole British brigade a further ten days to accomplish what one NSR company was supposed to achieve on D-Day.

Delay in fighting through heavy defences beyond the beach meant that the NSR did not join in the march inland on D+1, and therefore liberated few villages in the first days ashore. By the time it joined its brigade around Anguerny late on June 7, the front was already beginning to settle along lines the Canadians would hold for the next month. Holding the line therefore characterized the NSR's first month ashore. Much of that duty was grim, especially the period at le Mesnil-Patry, but it made combat veterans out of the men.

The real test of its skill and endurance, however, came at Carpiquet in early July. This battle is remembered in Canadian lore as a general failure with no redeeming features. The NSR experience at Carpiquet reveals a different story, one in which the Canadians gave as good as they got; one in

which the old North Shore, with a little help from its friends, destroyed the German operational reserve for the Caen sector and opened the way for the liberation of that key Normandy city.

Will R. Bird, who wrote the history of the regiment, comments that the NSR were largely a forgotten unit, even within the Canadian Army. The NSR "did not have equal representation at brigade or division head-quarters," Bird observed, "with the result that lesser units were given publicity and received the awards." His words reflect the views of the regiment itself and with some justification. In the many books on D-Day and Canada's role in the subsequent battle for Normandy published over the years, little is said of the NSR. Nor is there much commemoration in France today of its passing. The monuments on the esplanade in St. Aubin record its dead on D-Day and talk of how the NSR opened the way so the Royal Marine Commandos could liberate the town. Its actual landing beaches are unmarked, and the Hotel New Chatham is now *le Crabbe Verte* restaurant. The tiny hameau of Tailleville honoured the North Shore by naming its major crossroads Place du Royal North Shore Regiment and erecting a monument to one NSR soldier who was wounded in the village. What the North Shore accomplished at Carpiquet is unrecognized in Canadian military history and unrecorded in the Army's photographic collection. Small plaques on three small monuments, all with cryptic passages, record their heroism in early July 1944.

The Old North Shore deserves much better. This little book is a modest attempt to tell its story.

Chapter One

Origins

Military service in northern New Brunswick is as old as European settlement of the area. Those who manned the earliest French outposts established by Nicholas Denys in the seventeenth century were accustomed to bearing arms and fighting. The Acadian farmers who settled the region were part of the colonial militia of New France, whether they knew it or not. Some served in the defence of Fort Beauséjour in 1755 and in Boishébert's campaign of resistance against the British that followed. Acadians manned a gun battery where Campbellton now stands during the Battle of the Restigouche in 1760 and helped defend the Enclosure on the Miramichi. Even the Scots, Irish, and French Protestants who settled in the region after 1763 had experience either with war or military service. But no one could have imagined that when the Northumberland Battalion was established in 1787, it would be more than 150 years before the first formed unit from the North Shore engaged in combat. And no one could have imagined that when that day came, it would be in the leading wave of one of the greatest battles in history.

The long road to the D-Day landings at St. Aubin-sur-Mer, France, on June 6, 1944, began with the *Militia Act* of 1787, which obliged every county in New Brunswick to have one or more battalions of infantry.

The resulting Northumberland Battalion encompassed present-day Northumberland, Kent, Restigouche, and Gloucester counties. The colonial militia system was a rudimentary way of organizing and, if necessary, calling to arms the able-bodied men between the ages of sixteen and fifty to defend their homes. The strength of this "embodied militia" was a simple reflection of population, and officers and non-commissioned officers held their positions largely as a result of local social or economic standing. Training was non-existent, and the compulsory annual muster was simply a way to update the rolls. This was invariably a great social event and often notable for the amount of liquor consumed. No one really expected anything more.

In times of protracted crisis, British colonial governments raised fencible battalions, semi-permanent forces equipped for service within the colony itself but not part of the regular army. During the war with republican France in the 1790s, the King's New Brunswick Regiment (Fencibles) was raised, drawing on recruits from the various militia battalions. It was disbanded in 1802 when peace was signed with France. However, just a year later, when tensions with France rose again, the New Brunswick fencible battalion was raised. It included a body of men from the Northumberland Battalion. In 1810, the New Brunswick Fencibles were added to the regular order of battle of the British Army, becoming the 104th Regiment of Foot, a highly unusual distinction.

While the 104th Regiment garrisoned key sites in the province, the New Brunswick colonial militia grew steadily in response to the constant state of war with France. By 1809, a second Northumberland battalion had been formed at Richibucto, and in 1810 a third battalion of six companies — largely Acadian with Acadian officers — was established in Bathurst. The First Battalion along the Miramichi, with seven companies, remained one of the largest and, in David Facey-Crowther's words, "one of the most efficient of the provincial units." When tension with the United States grew in early 1812, Major John Kellock and two hundred Northumberland militiamen marched to Fredericton in the depths of winter to help defend the province. That feat was repeated a year later. When war broke out with the Americans in 1812, the 104th was one of the few British units within marching distance of the embattled frontier of Upper Canada, and so, in the winter of 1813, the soldiers marched up the St. John River on snowshoes, drawing their equipment on toboggans, on their way to Quebec and ultimately Kingston. Despite extremely cold weather averaging around -30°C and deep snow, only one man became sick and died. After a march of 1,128 kilometres, the 104th reached Kingston in mid-April without further loss.

The 104th was the only New Brunswick unit to see action in the War of 1812. Four companies of the regiment participated in the raid on the American naval base at Sackett's Harbour, just across Lake Ontario from Kingston, in May 1813. In 1814, the 104th joined in the Niagara campaign, fighting the battle of Lundy's Lane on July 25 and the ill-fated siege of Fort Erie later that summer. As a result of these actions and the involvement of some of its men, the Northumberland Battalion assumed the battle honour "Niagara" (it was never formally awarded). Meanwhile, the battalions at home worked hard to secure the province against attack. The 2nd Battalion, which included a large number of Acadians, built a blockhouse at the entrance to the Richibucto River and established a company of Sea Fencibles for service aboard ships. Fortunately, none of the twenty-three infantry battalions, several artillery batteries or the cavalry regiment of the New Brunswick Militia — 14,864 all ranks — was called upon to defend the province against American attack.

In the aftermath of the War of 1812 and the final defeat of Napoleon in 1815, the traditional colonial militia system expanded as the province grew, new counties were established, and new battalions were added to the militia. Kent County was established in 1826, and two years later, the 2nd Battalion of the Northumberland Militia became the 1st Battalion Kent County Militia. Gloucester County was established in 1828, but it was not until 1829 that its own militia was founded with the 1st Battalion in Bathurst and 2nd Battalion in Caraquet. When Restigouche County emerged in 1839, its 1st Battalion was established at Dalhousie. Meanwhile, the Northumberland Militia — always the strongest in numbers — had battalions at Chatham, Newcastle, Blackville, and Derby by the 1840s.

The provincial militia flourished in the 1820s and 1830s, largely because of the enduring problem of the boundary with the new state of Maine. With the settlement of that dispute in 1842 and improved relations with the United States, the militia went into sharp decline, until by the late 1840s it was virtually moribund. In 1851, the province suspended the sections of the *Militia Act* that provided for annual paid training periods. Defence of the empire, it was believed, was an imperial responsibility. The renewal of the suspension in 1856 for a further five years effectively killed the old colonial militia system in the province.

In place of the militia system, a volunteer system based on a new British model was established in the province, in which men formed units that met weekly for training on their own time and at their own expense. The movement spread to the colonies in the late 1850s, as groups of patriotic citizens formed volunteer companies within the existing battalion structures. In 1859, two of these volunteer units were formed in New Brunswick, the Havelock Rifles of Saint John and the Chatham Rifles drawn from the 1st Battalion Northumberland Militia. The provincial government supported the new movement, albeit reluctantly, due to pressure from Sir Arthur Hamilton Gordon, the lieutenant governor, and the public. In January 1860, a Military General Order authorized distribution of the latest Enfield rifles and accoutrements to "all Companies of the Regiments and Battalions under their commands which have volunteered or may volunteer for Drill." Perhaps because rifles were much more accurate and had a far greater range than the standard smooth bore musket, volunteer rifle companies and corps soon sprang up all over the province. The Miramichi Volunteer Rifle Company at Blackville and the Gloucester Rifle Corps in Bathurst were both established in 1860, and a rifle company followed at Dalhousie in 1861. According to Will Bird, despite regulations restricting their use to authorized military activities, soon "the carrying of rifles on practically all hunting expeditions" became the norm. Perhaps for that reason, northern militiamen fared well in the annual musketry competitions that started at Camp Sussex in 1861.

By 1867, the year of Canadian Confederation, virtually every battalion of the old militia had an active volunteer rifle company. As a result, the new *Militia Act of Canada* in 1868 established a system based on volunteer militia. In 1870, all volunteer companies on the Miramichi and North Shore were amalgamated into the 73rd (Northumberland) Battalion of the Canadian Militia. With its battalion-sized organization, the 73rd quickly became the dominant unit on the North Shore. Its first deployment was the despatch of forty-one officers and men to Caraquet in 1875 to maintain order in the wake of a riot. During the 1885 Northwest Rebellion on the Prairies, No. 1 Company was mobilized for service in the expeditionary force. However, Riel's rebels were defeated before the men left the province. Indeed, the only fighting the 73rd was involved in during the late nineteenth century were the recurring brawls in Moncton and Sussex with other provincial militiamen during training camps. When the Boer War erupted in 1899, a small number of men from the 73rd joined the New Brunswick contribution, G Company, of the 2nd (Special Service) Battalion of the Royal Canadian Regiment, although not in sufficient numbers to earn the battalion battle honours.

The fortunes of the 73rd improved by the turn of the twentieth century as the Canadian government modernized its militia. Even before the Boer War, the Canadian government had anticipated the possibility of overseas expeditionary forces, and it was important, therefore, to bring militia units up to speed in organization, equipment, and training. As a result, on May 8, 1900, the 73rd became the 73rd Northumberland Regiment, encompassing all the infantry units in Kent, Restigouche, Gloucester, and Northumberland counties. In 1911, when Canada agreed to adopt British organization for its army units, the 73rd was organized into two battalions, one based on the Miramichi and the other at Bathurst.

On August 4, 1914, as Britain and Germany drifted inexorably into war, the senior officers of the 73rd convened in Chatham and agreed to offer the services of the regiment to the empire, at home or abroad. Within days three companies had been called to active service to defend the wireless station at Newcastle. But the offer to mobilize the regiment was not accepted. Instead of fielding an expeditionary force based on Canada's militia units, as was called for by the staff plan, the Minister of Militia, Sam Hughes,

73rd Northumberland Regiment, Camp Sussex, NB, just before the Great War. Ken Wetherby

instituted a completely *ad hoc* system of battalions raised by local initiative. As a result, the 73rd sent its first drafts of men to the 12th Battalion formed at Camp Valcartier, Quebec, from Maritime and Quebec militia units. The 12th went overseas as a reserve battalion with the 1st Division but was disbanded in April 1915 to provide reinforcements for the front. Of all the battalions raised in New Brunswick during the Great War, only the 26th became operational. It served in the 5th Brigade of the 2nd Canadian Division. Two other battalions mobilized early on in the province, the 55th (NB and PEI) and the 64th (NB and NS), had cadres of North Shore men in them but were quickly broken up overseas for reinforcements.

Once the government's recruiting system became clearer, a concerted effort was made by the North Shore to get a battalion of its own into the ranks of the Canadian Expeditionary Force. The 132nd (North Shore) Battalion, raised in 1915 under Lieutenant-Colonel G.W. Mersereau, was really the core of the 73rd, with A Company from Campbellton, B Company from Chatham, C Company from Newcastle, and D Company from Bathurst. The recruiting drive was successful, and in October 1916, the 132nd sailed overseas at full strength. But it, too, was broken up to supply the insatiable needs of the units at the front. Later attempts fared no better: the 145th (NB and PEI) and the 165th (French-Acadian) both got to England only to be broken up. In the event, whole companies of men from New Brunswick reinforced units that had local affiliations elsewhere in Canada. When the 132nd was disbanded, 253 men went to the 26th (NB), but 182 filled the depleted ranks of the 42nd Battalion from Montreal, 340 went to the 87th from Ottawa, and 26 to the 78th from Winnipeg. Many others from the 145th, 165th, 64th, and 55th went to Quebec battalions. Anglophones joined battalions like the 5th Canadian Mounted Rifles from Quebec City, who had been virtually wiped out on the Somme in 1916, while Acadians went to the only francophone battalion at the front, the 22nd (the famous Van Doos). Eventually, protests from New Brunswick about the under-representation of its effort at the front led to the redesignation of the 44th (Brandon) Battalion as the 44th (NB) in August 1918; men from the North Shore served in that battalion, too.

The 73rd Northumberland Regiment was not unique in having no battalion serving overseas during the Great War: 250 battalions were recruited for the Canadian Expeditionary Force, but the 1st Canadian Corps only employed fifty. So when the numbered battalions of the Canadian Corps came home in 1918-1919, the government devised a scheme to distribute battle honours to militia regiments based on a minimum of 250 men from their area serving in specific engagements. The 73rd was granted Arras 1917 (which includes Vimy), Hill 70, Amiens, Arras 1918, Hindenburg Line, and Pursuit to Mons. Militia units were also reorganized to perpetuate the Canadian Expeditionary Force battalions. And so when in May 1920 the 73rd was redesignated the Northumberland (NB) Regiment, it perpetuated the 132nd, 145th, and 165th battalions.

Changes in name and organization in 1920 proved short-lived. In April 1921, a committee of officers, led by commanding officer Lieutenant-Colonel Cuthbert Donald, decided on, among other things, a new name and appropriate badges for the regiment. When new Regimental Orders were issued for 1922, they bore the name The North Shore Regiment. Badges had to wait until 1926. Meanwhile, infantry units in New Brunswick were reorganized further in 1922, drawing them together under the umbrella of The New Brunswick Regiment. According to the new mobilization plan for future overseas contingents, active units raised in New Brunswick were now to be battalions of the provincial regiment. For the time being, however, local militia units like the North Shore were to retain their names, organization, and identity. In the end, the ambitious plans for a large post-war army lapsed, as did the idea of mobilizing battalions of the notional New Brunswick Regiment for active service.

Like all other militia units, the North Shore Regiment survived the inter-war years and especially the Great Depression largely on the resolve of the officers and men to continue soldiering. After the stock market crash of 1929, the government provided only eight days of paid training a year and made no provision for summer camps. The NSR endured by pooling its meagre pay to cover the costs of transportation and some basics, and organizing its own summer camps at Salmon Beach. The regiment supplemented rations by sending some of its fishermen out daily to catch cod and mackerel. Since much basic infantry skill was fieldcraft, it was often difficult to make training interesting for the largely rural members of the regiment who, in addition to their farming, fishing, and lumbering work, were usually skilled hunters. Nonetheless, there was much to learn in drill and deportment, military organization and sanitation.

As things improved during the 1930s, camps moved back to Sussex, where the NSR could pit their skill — and occasionally their fists — against other militia units. There, as Will Bird observed, they won the Infantry Association Cup "often enough to consider themselves among the better units." They also won their share of brawls, typically against the NSR's arch rivals, The Carleton-York Regiment (CYR) from the upper Saint John River valley. According to regimental lore, these altercations were often orchestrated by The New Brunswick Rangers, the infantry regiment from the south of the province. During at least one such brawl, however, the cheering of the Rangers proved so hearty that the NSR and CYR stopped their fighting and turned together to administer a lesson to the instigators. It was, perhaps, the only time the North Shore and the CYR fought alongside one another. Both would soon have their fill of combat, but largely in different theatres of war.

As war loomed in the late summer of 1939, the NSR found itself fulfilling the same kinds of tasks the old 73rd had performed a generation earlier in August 1914: local guard duty, this time around bridges and armouries. Many thought that Lieutenant-Colonel J.A. Leger's refusal of the offer that summer to mobilize for coast defence was a "dangerous gamble," which might cause the regiment to be overlooked again for active service. The New Brunswick Rangers accepted the coastal defence job instead and spent much of their war in local garrison duty as a result. Meanwhile, the NSR's rivals, the Carleton and Yorks, mobilized for war in early September and soon went overseas as part of the 1st Division, taking with them a large number of men from the North Shore Regiment. That left only the NSR among New Brunswick infantry units without an active wartime role at the end of 1939. But Leger's gamble paid off. On May 24, 1940, with the German army pouring across Holland, Belgium, and northern France, the NSR was mobilized and, on June 5, assigned to the 8th Brigade of the 3rd Canadian Infantry Division.

The 1st Battalion, North Shore Regiment, on parade in England,
July 1941. 2RNBR

Chapter Two

The Long Road to St. Aubin

The mobilization of the North Shore Regiment for active service on May 24, 1940, was simply the start of a long road to war. With British forces retreating from the continent and France about to capitulate, the primary role of the Canadians for the foreseeable future was guarding Britain against invasion. In time, the 1st Canadian Army would switch roles and spearhead the Allied plans to return to the European continent. The most direct route to Germany from the west lay across the plains of northern France and Belgium. This campaign would be the culmination of the war in the west, and the NSR was destined to be part of it from start to finish. In the meantime, however, it would be four long years, almost to the day, before the NSR landed in France, and arduous years of preparation lay ahead.

As the regiment recruited to full strength (twenty-three officers and 949 other ranks) in early June 1940, the men had no uniforms, equipment, weapons, or place to assemble. Newcastle recruits were quartered in the curling rink and issued ill-fitting and poorly made denim clothing. The first days of training consisted of marching and physical exercises. In mid-June, the regiment moved to Woodstock, to the Island Park Camp developed by the CYR for their mobilization training the year before. "It was there in the middle of the

The North Shore Regiment marching through Woodstock in the summer of 1940. Carleton County Historical Society

[St. John River] river," Major J.A.L. Robichaud later recalled, "that we began our training as an infantry regiment, there also on that island that was cemented the real esprit de corps which characterized the North Shore Regiment." Robichaud was impressed by the ethnic harmony that prevailed in the regiment, although there was some friendly rivalry between the anglo companies (A from Chatham, B from Newcastle, and C from Campbellton) and D, the designated "French" company from Bathurst. Even the large number of local Native peoples who joined the NSR fit in easily with the farmers, woodsmen, and fishermen of mixed ethnicity who filled the rank and file. Indeed, the NSR retained that strong sense of local identity that characterized the regiment during its early years and would see it through difficult days ahead.

In December 1940, the battalion moved to Camp Sussex, familiar surroundings now being rapidly transformed into a major pre-deployment training and concentration base for formations going overseas. There the NSR met the other members of their brigade: The Queen's Own Rifles

The Sergeants' Mess, Camp Sussex, Winter 1941. Front row: Web McRae, Tom Sullivan, Bill Dickie, Earl Murray, Ray Young, and "Pitprop" the mascot. Standing: Arnold Devereaux, John Taylor, Jamie Chaisson, Hubert Carrier, Hector McNeill, Charlie Clarke, John Craig, Fred Moar, Frank Daley, Jim Richardson, Vince Dance, Jim Nugent, Jim Morrell, Gerald Moran, Clay Lynch, Bryden Weeks, Art Parsons, unknown, Frank Fraziee, Dan Godbout. Fred Moar

(QOR) from Toronto and Le Régiment de la Chaudière from Quebec. The QOR was the regiment of Toronto high society, officered by the educated and the well connected. Their sense of entitlement soon earned them the nickname "Christ's Own Rifles" among the men from New Brunswick. The Chauds, recruited from the rural villages and farms of the Chaudière River valley south of Quebec City, were as different from the QOR as chalk is from cheese. A solidly Québécois country battalion, the Chauds shared many of the same basic values and predilec-tions as the NSR but remained distinct by virtue of culture and — for many in the 8th Brigade — language. It was just as well per-haps that the 8th Brigade had many years to get to know one another before they were tested in combat.

It was in Sussex that Fenton Daley, later the NSR regimental sergeant-major, "realized we were no small-town heroes but just another spoke in a very large wheel." They arrived in winter while the base was under construction and conditions were hard. So, too, was the training when the spring came. As Daley remembered it, Sussex was ringed by hills "and I am sure we missed none of them." It was also in Sussex that the NSR showed its prowess at sports, winning the brigade hockey championship and excelling at baseball. And it was in Sussex that the first of the "overage" officers began to leave in the spring of 1941. Among them was Lieutenant-Colonel Leger, the battalion's much-loved CO, whose departure ended thirty years of soldiering. Captain J.E.H. LeBlanc later recalled that Leger was adored by the men, all of whom he knew by name, and that he "laid the foundation of . . . one of the finest fighting units in the Canadian army." He was replaced by Major J.R. Calkin, MC, a decorated veteran of the Great War, who was promoted to Lieutenant-Colonel.

On July 21, 1941, the 8th Brigade departed Halifax on the liner *Duchess of York* and arrived in Britain on the thirtieth. After disembarking in Liverpool, it went directly to Aldershot Camp to begin three long years of training and waiting. In the fall, it had its first exercise with tanks and live ammunition, and over that first winter, the NSR won the brigade and division hockey titles and narrowly lost the Canadian Corps title to the medical corps. In 1942, the regiment underwent some amphibious assault training and was on hand to watch the wreckage of the 2nd Canadian Division return from the ill-fated raid on Dieppe in August.

Apart from the endless training and route marches, the high point of 1942 for the NSR was probably the baseball season. Having already won the brigade and division championships, the ragtag team from the NSR, led by pitcher Jim Morrell of St. Stephen, faced the 5th Division champs, The Westminster Regiment, in the final for the Canadian Army trophy. When the ten members of the North Shore team arrived at Hove, on the south coast of England, they set off on foot to find the game site. Eventually they walked onto the pitch in front of five thousand fans to find the twenty-man Westminster side, all dressed in new white baseball uniforms, warming up. The crowd howled with derision at the tiny NSR team, dressed in old sweatshirts and shoes. They were much quieter when the NSR won seven to four. Embarrassed by the outcome, the 5th Division demanded a best-of-three final. When Morrell and his team returned, they, too, sported new uniforms and shoes, and the regimental band came along to support them. In the meantime, the Westminster team had morphed into the 5th Division All-Stars, with a number of semi-professional players in the lineup. But Morrell, a AAA ball player with hands like hams and a world-class pitching arm, held them to six runs, and the NSR put up eight to win the series and the warm cheers of the crowd. For the men of the North Shore, winning at baseball or hockey — or succeeding as soldiers — was all in a day's work.

In June 1942, the NSR received a new second-in-command, thirty-seven-year old Major D.B. Buell, a Permanent Force officer from The Royal Canadian Regiment. Three months later, on September 8, Buell was promoted to Lieutenant-Colonel and assumed command of the regiment from Calkin. It was Buell who took the NSR through its final training and preparation for battle, and its first and perhaps toughest period of fighting in France. It could not have hoped for a better leader. A graduate of the Royal Military College in 1922, Buell had made his career as a trainer and instructor in tactics, most recently at the officer cadet training school at Camp Borden. He knew how to train officers, and, as Fred Moar recalled, he knew how to train the battalion. These qualities and Buell's skill in tactics would serve the NSR very well in the days ahead.

In 1943, the seemingly relentless cycle of training and route marches was punctuated by a number of changes. In February, the Canadian Army briefly adopted the British model of three rifle companies per battalion rather than four. Buell used the opportunity to weaken the rivalries (not always positive) among the locally recruited companies. After consulting with his officers, Buell dispersed D Company, the French company, among the others. When, in July, the organization returned to four companies,

Lieutenant-Colonel G.S. Currie, Deputy Minister of Defence (Army), inspects the North Shore just prior to D-Day. The men are wearing the new helmets and high invasion boots (eliminating the need for putties) adopted by the assault troops. LAC e006581502

Buell shuffled the deck again and broke up the local affiliations even further. The result was a battalion that was a more uniform mixture of the whole North Shore region.

In 1943, the first NSR personnel were assigned to combat when several drafts of officers and NCOs were sent to serve with British units in North Africa and later with the 1st Canadian Division in Italy. In theory they were to gain much-needed practical experience and bring that back to their unit. Captain A.M. MacMillan and Company Sergeant-Major Fenton Daley saw three months of the war in North Africa and returned. But the second group to go in October, two captains, two lieutenants, and four sergeants, were simply treated as reinforcements and ended up lost to the regiment. The two lieutenants were killed, and the rest never returned to the NSR.

Training intensified in 1943 as it became clearer that the invasion of France had to happen soon and that the 3rd Canadian Division would be in the initial assault. Allied armies were ashore in Italy by September (including the Carleton and Yorks) and were nearing Rome by the fall; meanwhile the Russian summer offensive was carving a huge hole in the German defences in the east. In September, the 8th Brigade went north, to Inverary in Scotland, to train in earnest for its role in the amphibious assault on France. There, at the Combined Operations base, the NSR went to sea in the assault ship HMS *St. Helier* and trained loading into and landing from small boats called Landing Craft, Assault (LCA). Each LCA carried thirty men, was armoured against machine-gun fire, and was designed to put the men directly on the beach off a small ramp. The training at Inverary was conducted with the naval forces who would, on D-Day, land the NSR on the coast of France. Having mastered the basics, the NSR continued to practice amphibious assaults as the days wore down to the actual attack.

Final training over the fall and winter of 1943-44 included working closely with other formations and units the NSR would have to fight alongside. Among these were The 12th Field Regiment, Royal Canadian Artillery, tanks of The Fort Garry Horse from the 2nd

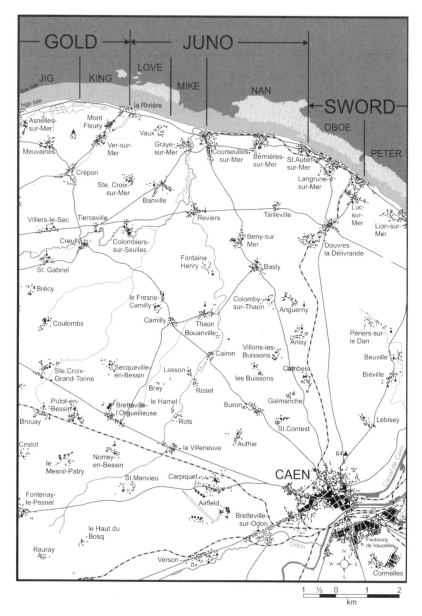

The North Shore Regiment's area of operations, June 6 to July 10, 1944. Mike Bechthold

Armoured Brigade, heavy machine guns and mortars of The Cameron Highlanders of Ottawa (MG), and the engineers and ambulance troops that would support the brigade in action. The training was progressive — moving from basic skills to increasing complexity and more units involved — and it was intense. Everyone in the 3rd Division knew what their task was: they had to get ashore and stay there. After General B.L. Montgomery, the officer in charge of the armies going ashore, informed the troops in early 1944 that he would accept seventy-five percent casualties to secure the landing site, no one was under any illusions about the job that lay ahead.

The challenge facing the Allies in Operation OVERLORD (the code name for the invasion of France) was daunting. The Germans had had nearly four years to prepare defences and, in the final months of 1943, had launched a major effort to make the likely landing sites around Calais and in the Baie de la Seine impenetrable. Massive coastal artillery batteries intended to destroy the invading armada were supplemented by smaller gun-in-concrete emplacements designed to sink landing craft as they approached. Machine-gun positions protected the guns and covered the beaches with fire, while mines, barbed wire, and obstructions built on the sand down to the low-water mark were meant to impede the movement of men, ships, and vehicles, making them easy targets. Farther back, mortar and artillery positions provided indirect fire onto the beaches, and high-velocity anti-tank guns and minefields guarded exit points. Behind the beach defences, mobile reserves were poised to counter-attack any Allied troops who managed to get ashore. It would have been an insurmountable fortress had the Germans commanded the air and sea, but by the spring of 1944 they did neither. That meant that the Atlantic Wall could be penetrated with the right combination of equipment, training, planning, and determination.

The Allied scheme for attacking this formidable fortress was complex and encompassed the whole European theatre. Deception and counter-intelligence operations played to German fears, especially of a landing in the Pas de Calais, and kept their 15th Army in place there. Indeed, uncertain about just where the Allies might land, afraid of Allied naval firepower, and confident of their own ability to launch massive counter-attacks, the Germans decided to keep their major reserve forces, especially the Panzer divisions, well back from the beach. It would take most of these formations a day or more to reach any landing site. Meanwhile, in early 1944, an assault began on German air power with the intent of destroying it in the west: this was accomplished by the end of March. And starting in April, Allied bomber forces systematically destroyed the French railway and road system, isolating the landing sites and making it difficult for the Germans to move their armoured reserves forward quickly. Finally, in May, the Allies began a massive attack on German positions south of Rome, hoping to siphon off enemy formations and reserves from the French front.

All of this was far beyond the immediate concerns of the North Shore and other assault battalions preparing to land in France. Its job was to breach the coastal fortress and establish a lodgement that would allow the Allies to build a huge army ashore. The final assault plan called for the landing of more than eight divisions along the southern coast of the Baie de la Seine between the Orne River and the base of the Cotentin Peninsula. To the west of Bayeux, four American seaborne divisions, two airborne divisions and elements of several others were slated to land on either side of the Vire River estuary. East of the Americans, three beaches and one air-landing zone were assigned to the 2nd British Army, which included the 3rd Canadian Division. The British 6th Airborne Division (including the 1st Canadian Parachute Battalion) was to capture the high ground east of Caen and the bridges over the Orne River and Caen Canal in order to secure the eastern flank of the British assault beaches. These included the British 3rd Division on Sword Beach, just west of the Orne estuary. It had the extremely difficult task of capturing Caen, the hub of road and rail communications in lower Normandy. Gold Beach, north of Bayeux, was assigned to the British 50th Division, which was tasked with the capture of that city. In between Gold and Sword, the 3rd Canadian Division was to land on Juno Beach. The Canadian job was to cut the road and rail lines between Bayeux and Caen, and, since it occupied crucial ground, stop the expected German armoured counter-attack.

Juno Beach stretched for seven kilometres, from the seaside village of St. Aubin in the east to the dunes west of the Seulles River. Each of the villages hugging that shoreline — St. Aubin, Bernières, and Courseulles — were fronted by seawalls, and all had strongpoints and guns in bunkers just above the waterline. The strongest place by far on Juno Beach lay astride the Seulles River. The little harbour of Courseulles-sur-Mer was protected by massive concrete positions in the dunes west of the river and along the village seafront to the east, mounting some large guns. The job of cracking these defences fell to the 7th Canadian Infantry Brigade. The Royal Winnipeg Rifles and a company of 1st Battalion The Canadian Scottish Regiment would land west of the river on beaches code-named Mike Green and Mike Red, while The Regina Rifle Regiment would land directly in front of Courseulles on Nan Green. The Courseulles defences were among the toughest confronted by any Allied soldiers on D-Day; however, once across the beach and through the village, there was little behind to stop the 7th Brigade's advance inland.

The rest of the Canadian assault on Juno Beach fell to the 8th Brigade, which also planned to attack on a two-battalion front. The Queen's Own Rifles, the "senior" battalion of the brigade, got the nod for the landing on the right on Nan White. The beach directly in front of Bernières-sur-Mer was defended by a strongpoint with two 50-mm guns and several supporting machine guns atop a six-foot-high seawall, flanked by minefields and with a deep anti-tank ditch behind the eastern sector. The QOR plan was to land east and west of the village along a stretch of dune and capture Bernières from the flanks. As was the case with the 7th Brigade beach, once through the seafront defence, there were no major second-line positions behind Bernières.

Further to the east, the beach in front of the 8th Brigade's other initial objective, St. Aubin, was simply unassailable. The village lay, just as it does today, hard by the sea, atop a ten-foot-high wall. In 1944, the buildings

The strongpoint at St. Aubin. Zigzag lines indicate trenches; lines of *X*s are barbed wire; square blocks are concrete positions; square blocks with arrows are 50-mm guns in concrete; plain arrows indicate suspected or known machine guns; the large arrow with the line through it and a "2" is the sight of the two 75-mm field guns, while a similar arrow on the road to the right is an anti-tank gun. The large *X* on the beach road and the smaller one on the left in the street running up from the beach (on the Rue Canet, see photo on p 56) are roadblocks. The church is in the upper left. NBM

were fortified with machine guns, and 20-mm anti-aircraft guns dotted the roofs at one-hundred-metre intervals. The beach and the main road along the seafront was covered by three 50-mm anti-tank guns in concrete positions built into the seawall (one is still there), two 75-mm guns, and concrete machine-gun posts. All beach exits in the village were blocked and covered with interlocking fire from many guns, and the roads by the sea were barricaded, choked with telephone poles laid in the streets to impede tank movement.

Dominating the beach in front of St. Aubin was what the Germans called *Wiederstandneste* (WN) 27, the strongpoint on the promontory of Cap Romain. Here, in a complex of bunkers, trenches, barbed wire and fortified stone buildings, were the two 75-mm guns in an open emplacement and two 50-mm anti-tank guns in concrete positions that controlled the beach in front of St. Aubin. Another 50-mm gun in an open emplacement faced west, and all these guns, including two 81-mm mortars, were guarded by five steel-reinforced concrete pillboxes, numerous other machine guns, and a garrison variously estimated at between forty and ninety men. The Germans demolished buildings behind Cap Romain to clear fields of fire around the strongpoint and sowed extensive minefields to protect it and the beaches. With twenty-foot cliffs on the seaward side, Cap Romain acted like a tower on a castle wall: its fire could sweep the beach directly in front of St. Aubin and the more open stretch to the west in front of the hamlet of la Rive Plage.

Capture of the seaside village of St. Aubin was the primary target of the left-hand assault battalion of the 8th Brigade: whoever drew that assignment also got the toughest task of any single Canadian battalion to land on D-Day. The actual landing zone, designated Nan Red, lay just west of the Cap Romain strongpoint, in front of the hamlet of la Rive (then, as now, actually part of the village of Bernières). The beach itself was guarded by an offshore reef that was impassable at low tide and a strong west-east tidal stream. As with all other Atlantic Wall beaches, the intertidal zone of Nan Red was filled with obstacles. As far to seaward as possible, the

Germans erected two rows of "Element C" obstacles (structures that looked like a huge gate), backed by several rows of wooden stakes with mines attached to the tops. Closer to shore was a double row of hedgehogs: three steel bars, like railway tracks, welded into a large, three-legged *X*. Behind all this, the beach itself was barred by barbed wire and minefields, stretching along seawalls and dunes, and covered by fire from fortified emplacements and beachfront houses.

Nan Red ran for roughly a kilometre west of the present day Rue de la Libération, which constituted the western edge of the strongpoint and is still the boundary between St. Aubin and Bernières. At this point the sandstone cliffs of Cap Romain start to fall away. In 1944, the low bluffs ended at a seafront château that jutted out onto the beach and was protected from the sea on three sides by a low stone seawall. Nothing whatsoever remains of this château and its seawall. Just to the west of the château lay 160 yards of open beach, fronted by dunes and free of buildings. This open beach ran back one hundred yards to the coastal road. Photographic evidence indicated that the Germans used this gap to access their beach defences. Allied planners labelled it N.7, a major beach exit for the build-up phase. It is now a seaside park. Beyond the gap further west, in front of la Rive, was a low seawall cloaked in spools of barbed wire. The seawall was not high, perhaps six feet, and the row of houses and villas just behind it — a dozen in all — were spaced out, with good gaps in between them and only a smattering of structures behind. Once through this veneer, the ground behind this portion of la Rive Plage was open country. In short, the gap and the beach at la Rive could be penetrated.

Intelligence determined that the seafront from St. Aubin to Bernières was held by elements of the 5th Company of the 736th Battalion, 716th (Coastal) Division. The Germans rated the 716th a good division for static defence: the Canadians rated it as worth about forty percent of the fighting value of a first-class division. A very rough estimate of the German garrison at Nan Red and the strongpoint on Cap Romain was less than one hundred men, with about forty estimated to be in the strongpoint itself. The German defenders at St. Aubin and la Rive were assisted by an uncertain number of *Osttruppen*, soldiers captured in

Russia and enlisted into German service. The Allies did not expect these men to fight hard, if at all.

The beach defences of Nan Red differed in detail from those faced by the other Canadian battalions on D-Day, but they were not unique. What made Nan Red particularly tough was what lay behind it. South of St. Aubin, across two kilometres of open farmland, lay the tiny village of Tailleville. It was fortified, and intelligence received by mid-May indicated extensive work on a major infantry strongpoint, with machine guns and an anti-tank gun in concrete positions, elaborate trenches and underground shelters, and at least four 88-mm guns sited to cover "approaches from the coast." What lay in the large forested area immediately south of Tailleville was unclear.

More alarming still was the huge radar complex — the biggest in Normandy — southeast of Tailleville, near Douvres-la-Délivrande. This was a two-part complex. The northern section, closest to Tailleville, contained three massive concrete bunkers for three 20-mm anti-aircraft guns. This position was protected in turn by concrete machine-gun positions, trenches, minefields, and extensive barbed wire. Across the road to the south, the main radar complex consisted of a massive five-story underground concrete structure surrounded by its own concrete machine-gun and mortar positions, trenches, and mines. In all, the radar station held six 50-mm anti-tank guns, one 75-mm field gun, sixteen machine guns, several heavy mortars, and 240 men, all wrapped inside belts of wire and steel-reinforced concrete. No other Canadian D-Day beach had such strong inland obstacles behind it.

By rights, the honour of tackling Nan Red should have gone to the Chaudières, the second most senior battalion of the 8th Brigade. But the NSR had done exceptionally well in its training, and Buell claimed that his battalion was one of the top two in the whole army. To prove that, in January 1944, A Company won the award for the best company in the 3rd Division following a gruelling "Efficiency Competition." Having already beaten the best of the 8th Brigade, A Company found the rest of the competition

A Company's beach. Gap N.7 is to the left. NBM

fairly easy. The men were exceptionally fit, motivated, and well trained as soldiers. Indeed, after the division competition finished in the darkness of a cold English January evening, the company marched twenty-five miles in quick time in order to get home for a dance. The success of A Company in the competition may well have determined which of the other two battalions of the brigade would land in the assault wave. The NSR drew the assault role for Nan Red, relegating the Chaudières as the reserve battalion.

A Company's success also meant that forty-two-year-old Major J.A. "Archie" McNaughton could stay to lead his company in battle. Tagged as too old for combat duty, Buell had routinely urged him to retire from active service. "You did enough in the Great War," the men of the NSR would say to him. But the farmer and fish warden from Black River was the "most loved and respected officer in the battalion" and the "father of "A" Company." McNaughton had taken most of the NSR troublemakers and moulded them into a band of men who would follow him anywhere. They proved that in the Efficiency Competition, and in doing so, the men of A Company ensured that McNaughton would lead them on D-Day.

Serious planning for the assault began in March 1944, when maps, terrain models, and aerial photos — none of them using the real place names — became available. Based on these, Buell and his officers, in consultation with their supporting units, developed a multi-phased and highly ambitious plan for D-Day. The first phase was to secure a beach-head. This would be done by landing on a two-company front astride the gap, N.7, west of the strongpoint. A Company would land in front of la Rive and move inland to secure the southwestern approaches to St. Aubin and make contact with the QOR at Bernières. B Company would land on the east side of the gap, around the château, breach the beach defences and then turn to capture the strongpoint. C Company would land behind A and occupy the southern outskirts of St. Aubin around the railway station and church. Meanwhile, D Company was to come ashore behind B, move inland and then swing east to capture the main part of St. Aubin village.

B Company's beach. Gap N.7 is to the right, the strongpoint to the left. NBM

The second phase of Buell's plan was a succession of leaps by companies. C Company, supported by A, was to seize Tailleville. Then A Company would take the forest south of Tailleville, which would serve as a staging area for D Company's assault on the radar station. Once that was all done, late in the day the battalion would advance to the high ground around Anguerny and form a solid front with the rest of the 8th Brigade.

The North Shore were not expected to do this all alone. Every conceivable effort was made to destroy or neutralize the defences prior to their landing and support the NSR ashore. Getting safely off the beach was especially critical. The landing was scheduled for low tide to avoid impaling the landing craft on the beach obstacles and permit engineers to clear lanes to the beach exits before the tide came in. As a result, the infantry had to cross one hundred yards or more of open sand before they reached the comparative shelter of the beach or seawall. Most beaches were bombed during the night by the British, but no aerial attack on St. Aubin was slated until first light, when the strongpoint was to be struck by American bombers. Then, forty minutes before touchdown, the Norwegian destroyer *Glaisdale* would fire on Cap Romain, followed ten minutes later by all twenty-four guns of the 19th Field Regiment, RCA, firing 120 rounds per gun from their landing craft and the entire arsenal, a thousand 27-kilogram rockets, of one Landing Craft, Tank (Rocket). As the infantry moved in, large landing craft equipped with heavy guns would move with them on either flank and small gunships would beach on Nan Red itself to fire at enemy positions.

If all that was not enough, the NSR had formidable tank support. Shortly before the scheduled infantry landing, swimming tanks of the Fort Garry Horse were to arrive and open fire on the defences from positions awash in the surf. Then, just in front of the infantry, Armoured Vehicles, Royal Engineers (AVREs) were to arrive. These were equipped with flails — heavy chains on a drum mounted in front of the tank — that beat their way through wire and mines, and "Dustbin" mortars firing heavy, shaped charges to destroy concrete emplacements, assisted by armoured bull-

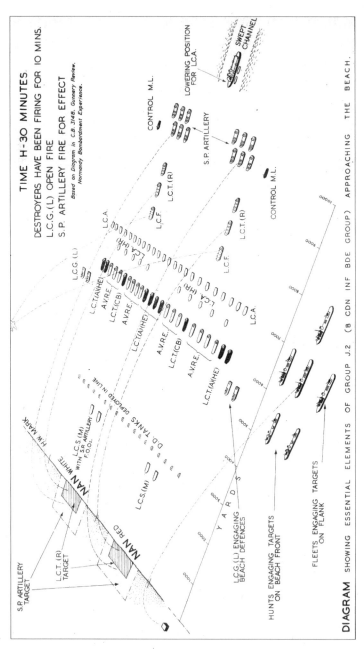

DIAGRAM SHOWING ESSENTIAL ELEMENTS OF GROUP J.2 (8 CDN INF BDE GROUP) APPROACHING THE BEACH.

A notional representation of the plan for landing the two assault battalions of the 8th Canadian Infantry Brigade on Nan beach. Note that the infantry in their LCAs were in the third wave, led by DD tanks swimming ashore, and specialized Armoured Vehicles, Royal Engineers (AVRE). LCMSDS dozers. Buell also had with him a Forward Officer, Bombardment from the British destroyer *Vigilant*, whom he could call on for help, while Forward Observation Officers (FOOs) from The 19th Field Regiment were available to call for support from self-propelled artillery joining the assault. Initially this fire was to come from the 90-mm howitzers of the Centaur self-propelled guns of the 2nd Royal Marine Assault Squadron (RMAS). They would stop in hull-down positions in the surf and, directed by the FOOs, support the battle for the beach and village. Once the beach was secure, the self-propelled guns of the 19th RCA would start to arrive as well, as would the 48th Royal Marine Commandos, who would pass through the Canadians to attack east towards Langrune-sur-Mer. At the same time, combat engineers would arrive to clear obstacles, open the exit, and prepare the beach for follow-up troops. In short, while Nan Red was the North Shore's beach, the attack was a complex and highly sophisticated combined-arms assault, and they would get a great deal of help.

In early April, the NSR moved to Chilworth, just outside Southampton on the Channel coast, and on the twelfth the men sent all their surplus clothes and personal effects to long-term storage. A number of final exercises followed to ensure that men could get on and off landing craft efficiently, that the navy could coordinate operations, and that men, tanks, and their supporting weapons were able to get inland quickly. By mid-May, their camp was sealed, encircled by barbed wire, and patrolled by armed American guards: no one got in or out.

Major (later Brigadier) Ernie Anderson recalled that on May 18, Buell took all the company commanders into the middle of a field and told them they were going to France. By that stage, they had studied aerial photos of their landing sites and maps with fictitious names applied. However, it was not until they were onboard the assault ships in Southampton on June 5, 1944, after a day's delay due to bad weather, that the NSR finally found out where it was bound. As Padre Hickey wrote, "Major Lockwood, second in command of the regiment, came into the officers quarters [of the

assault ship *Brigadier*, which carried the regimental headquarters] and said 'It's on!'. . . The tense days of guessing and secrecy were over. Maps were unrolled — and there was our landing place, St. Aubin-sur-Mer, a tiny village on the French coast. At that moment St. Aubin was living in blessed obscurity; another day, and its name would be flashed around the world." Later that day, the vast armada departed, and, as Father Hickey so eloquently observed, "a half million men sailed out to meet the scarlet dawn." For the men of the North Shore (NB) Regiment, the long road to St. Aubin — the long road to war — was about to end.

Chapter Three

D-Day

Dawn comes early in the northern latitudes in June, and Normandy, which lies as far north as Labrador, is no exception. The landings in the American zone started at 0630 hours, and then spread eastward with the rising tide. When Lieutenant-Colonel Buell and his officers caught their first glimpse of Nan Red, they were still miles offshore and more than an hour away from touchdown. The grey sea was rough, the wind raw, and low storm clouds scudded overhead against solid overcast. All around them lay a vast invasion armada. "As far as I could see," Major Ernie Anderson of D Company wrote later, "there was a solid mass of ships." Yellow-orange flashes of naval gunfire lit up the sky as the small assault vessels wallowed in the heavy seas. The Landing Craft, Tank (LCT) carrying the Shermans of the Fort Garry Horse pitched so steeply that Buell, looking down from the landing ship *Brigadier,* could "see right inside those nearest to us."

Gradually, as the "dark line on the southern horizon" took form, the men of the North Shore Regiment "recog-  nized salient features, the church steeple in Langrune, the water tower at St. Aubin." "All our landmarks were clearly visible," Buell recalled. At 0630 the men clambered down into their forty-one-foot-long LCAs for the one-hour run to the beach. The fumes from

8th Brigade infantry loaded into a Landing Craft, Assault during an exercise in the spring of 1944: these were the craft that carried the assault wave. LAC e006581365

the LCAs' engines and the rolling sea made most men immediately seasick. This much they had endured before. As Buell remarked, "the illusion persisted that this just another exercise." Even in the leading wave, the sentiment was much the same. Lieutenant C.F. Richardson of 11 Platoon, B Company, remembered the men singing as German tracers filled the air around them in the final approach: "everyone in our boat seemed to take it as just another scheme." But Nan Red was no exercise. It proved to be the toughest and longest fight of the day for any Canadian battalion, and by the evening, 124 of the old North Shore lay dead or wounded on the coast of France.

It is an old military axiom that no plan survives contact with the enemy, and Juno Beach was no exception. The weather upset the delicate timing of things from the outset. Landings were slated to begin at 0730, three hours before high tide, giving just enough water for landing craft to clear the offshore reefs, but not so high as to submerge the beach obstacles. However, the last vestiges of the storm that had delayed the attack by a day also made it impossible to get things just right. Few specific targets were struck by the naval bombardment, and the drenching fire from the artillery and rocket ships fell too far inland. All the navy ever promised was about twelve minutes of suppression of the beach defences, and on this they largely delivered.

The weather threw off the landing sequence as well. The tanks were supposed to arrive first, five minutes ahead of the infantry, and suppress the defences with their fire. But they were delayed and, in any event, could not be launched offshore to swim in because of the sea state. By the time the infantry landed, the tanks were still two thousand yards offshore. Of the thirty-two Centaurs of the 2nd Royal Marine Assault Squadron slated to help on the Canadian beach-

es, several were lost when three landing craft capsized in the heavy seas. Two other LCTs carrying Centaurs had to return to England; only twenty-two Centaurs actually landed on D-Day. Finally, the Churchill AVREs of the 5th Assault Squadron, Royal Engineers, who were supposed to clear the

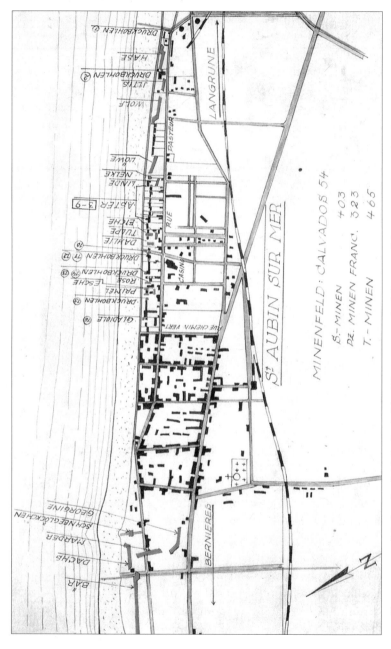

German map of their minefields in St. Aubin. The group on the left covered the strongpoint at Cap Romain. Ville de St. Aubin

beach exits for vehicles, including tanks, missed their landing sites and were late arriving.

ASSAULTING ST. AUBIN

As a result, the assault companies of the North Shore Regiment hit the beaches first and alone. A and B companies touched down east of the strongpoint and in front of la Rive at 0745, each with two platoons leading and one following. The beach was buzzing with enemy machine-gun fire. Both companies dashed across the one hundred metres of open sand from the LCAs to the comparative safety of the seawall and dune line. A Company suffered the worse. Nine Platoon lost three NCOs to a mine blast in the sprint to the seawall, the platoon commander, Lieutenant M.M. Keith, was seriously wounded, and nearly a whole section of ten men was wiped out when the charge set to blow a gap in the wire along the seawall detonated a hidden mine. Keith remained on the beach until the next morning, when he was literally picked up by a 240-pound British sailor who carried him on board a landing craft muttering, "I carried your bleeding fathers in World War I and now I'm carrying you!" While 9 Platoon poured through the gap in the wire blown by Keith, Lieutenant Fred Moar's 7 Platoon simply ran through a gap in the seawall caused by the naval bombardment. As Moar recalled, he never stopped running from the time he left the LCA until he was inside the seawall at la Rive. The beach was swept by machine-gun and mortar fire. "But we were the best assault company in the division and the defences in front of us were not a serious fortification," Moar stated.

Once across the seawall, one platoon of A Company pushed inland for the road behind and to establish contact with the QOR to their right. Corporal J.R. Currie's group lost five men getting over a high stone wall behind the first row of houses and then had to cut a belt of wire to get across the road in behind. The other platoons cleared the buildings up and down the beach. The seaside houses were booby-trapped, littered with mines, and filled

B Company's beach about mid-morning, D-Day. The seawall, against
which a number of bodies remain, belonged to the seaside château.
The banners raised behind the wall are markers for gap N.7. IWM

with Germans; this lethal combination caused most of A Company's
casualties that morning. It also earned Corporal F.S. Savage of 2 Platoon
a Military Medal for leading his section through a number of houses. By
the time Major Archie McNaughton and his headquarters party came
ashore in the fourth LCA, they were able to scramble quickly through
the beachfront and out to the coast road. It took an hour and a half of
nasty, house-to-house fighting to secure the beach at la Rive.

The leading platoons of B Company also got ashore without serious losses, although 4 Platoon suffered one man wounded before the
ramp even went down. Nonetheless, things started well. Lieutenant
Richardson and 4 Platoon landed on the company's right, directly in
front of the château with a very small stretch of seawall in front: "Once
we were out of the boat everyone acted mechanically, heading for the
beach and the cover of the beach wall." By all accounts, Richardson's platoon made it safely to the beach, cut the wire with explosives, and raced

inland through a minefield, and were soon "at close quarters with the enemy." Meanwhile, to the left of the château, Lieutenant G.V. Moran's 5 Platoon was soon trapped on the beach and suffering from mortar and machine-gun fire. Moran quickly realized that if they stayed there they would all die. "In order to get the men moving to their objective," Moran later recalled, he stood up, with his back to the beach, "and shouted at the top of my voice and, making vigorous motions with my arms, urged the sections around the wall and forward." His action got 5 Platoon moving just as a sniper's bullet ripped through his extended arm, into his chest and out his back. Moran had no idea he had been shot because at the same time he was blown flat by a mortar bomb.

Major Ernest Anderson and D Company reached the beach while much of B Company was still sheltering below the seawall. Their run in had been uneventful until two hundred yards out, when machine-gun fire began to lace the LCAs. By the time the door opened, "bullets were hitting like a hail storm on the water." Anderson did not recall anyone in his craft being hit on the dash across the beach, but Corporal Main simply disappeared: he was never seen again. The D Company commander arrived just in time to find Lieutenant Moran gravely wounded. After quickly grouping the wounded under the shelter of the seawall, Anderson, D Company, and the rest of B slipped inland along a "well worn path that must have been used by German beach parties." Within minutes D Company were behind the town at their rendezvous, where the main road through St. Aubin intersected the road to Tailleville. There they waited, enduring mortar fire from the strongpoint, before moving on to the railway station in preparation for their task of clearing the village.

Meanwhile, back near the beach, Lieutenant Paul McCann of B Company's 6 Platoon now found himself in command of Moran's platoon as well and confronting the strongpoint. Sheltered by steel-reinforced concrete and wire, and bristling with machine guns, the unseen Germans in the strongpoint directed mortar and machine-gun fire onto the beach and the vessels approaching. They also controlled all the landward approaches

to their position. "Perhaps it was well we didn't know everything" about the defences of St. Aubin before they landed, McCann remembered. For "working on the assumption that we had a pushover, we went into the village in nothing flat. Now came the test." For the time being they had nothing to work with except small arms and grenades. By the time Captain Bill Harvey, the B Company second in command, arrived, his platoons were all taking casualties, were making no progress in their attack on the strongpoint and no tanks had yet appeared.

In the meantime, in front of la Rive, C Company landed a few minutes behind A and crossed the beach with few casualties. The plan was to move quickly inland, and they did. Captain Hector LeBlanc, the second in command, cut a gap through the barbed wire along the seawall with his own cutters through which two of his platoons scrambled successfully. C Company's third platoon found its own gap in the wire and lost three men getting through. With these modest losses, C Company soon rendezvoused with its commander, Major R.H. Daughney, then moved south to their assigned objective around the church on the south side of St. Aubin. Up to this point, the only direct fire support the NSR had received came from several of the navy's Landing Craft, Gun, which pushed in close to the beach. Their fire knocked out at least one gun in the strongpoint.

By the time the reserve companies began to move inland, the first tanks of the Fort Garry Horse arrived. They were late. According to the plan, the amphibious Shermans of C Squadron were supposed to launch ten thousand yards out, swim in, and arrive first. From hull-down positions in the surf, they were to engage the defences while the infantry landed all around them. But the Garrys had a dreadful time getting into action. Delayed by heavy seas, the "Duplex Drive" swimming tanks were launched a mere one thousand yards from shore in what was described as a wet wade. In the process, one LCT was struck by shellfire and another sank. Four of C Squadron's twenty tanks never made it to the beach.

Meanwhile, the AVREs that were supposed to land about the same time as the Garrys and clear a path through the obstacles and the beach exit were late, too. They and the Centaur self-propelled guns of Y and Z Troops of 2 RMAS only started to land at 0805. As it turned out, Nan

Red was the only beach where the 2 RMAS landing went well: six guns got ashore and into action, while most of the rest were either lost at sea or taken back to Britain when their landing craft were damaged.

Despite these setbacks, by shortly after 0800 Nan Red — already awash in wreckage, with bodies of the dead and wounded everywhere — was crawling with tanks and self-propelled guns. However, until the AVREs cleared a path through the obstacles and minefields, the Fort Garry tanks and 2 RMAS Centaurs had no where to go. Padre Myles Hickey, who spent two hours on that shell-torn strand saving the wounded and administering to the dead, wrote later that amid the din of battle no one could even hear the tanks. Men were crushed as the armoured vehicles manoeuvred and fired.

Fortunately, the Fort Garrys' C Squadron commander, Major William Bray, who won a DSO for his D-Day actions, understood what had to be done. After a few minutes of milling around, and after watching an armoured bulldozer pick away at the obstacles, Bray drove his tank towards the beach exit at N.7 and ordered the rest to follow. Sergeant Albanie Drapeau, in charge of the 3-inch mortars of the NSR support company, who had just struggled ashore with his handcart packed with the mortar and thirty bombs, watched the tanks go. "One tank came roaring in through the gap and struck a mine at once," Drapeau recalled. "A second one ran for it and reached the main street." The Garrys lost three tanks getting through the minefield or to anti-tank fire on the road, but the gap was now breached.

Forcing the exit allowed the Fort Garry tanks, as well as the Centaurs of 2 RMAS and the mortars of the NSR, to push inland. Drapeau and his mortar team dragged their cart up the track, found their assigned position behind the village, and soon were "laying a few rounds for ranging." The Bren carriers of the mortar platoon arrived shortly afterwards, by which time AVRE Flails had arrived to start clearing the exit. And while the Garrys' tanks turned to provide direct fire support to B and D Companies attacking the village and strongpoint, the Centaurs of 2 RMAS

deployed just west of St. Aubin and were soon firing in support, one of their barrages consisting of fifteen rounds per gun at a range of only 650 yards.

By about 0845 Buell had his first situation report at his headquarters near the church, and things were going reasonably well. C and the Support Company were consolidating around the church guarding the southern flank of the battalion, the mortar platoon was in action, A Company was about to reach its beachhead objective south of la Rive and make contact with the Queen's Own at Bernières, and D Company was poised near the train station to clear the town. Anticipating phase two of the operation, Buell now ordered his naval Forward Officer, Bombardment to have the destroyers offshore start firing on Tailleville. However, when he learned that B Company was making no progress against the strongpoint, Buell went back to the beach to see for himself what the problem was.

Buell arrived at the B Company positions just in time to witness the tragic landing of 48 Commando, Royal Marines. Carried in older, wooden landing craft from which they had to disembark on ramps hung from either side of the vessel, the Marines were supposed to come ashore on a secure beach, pass through the NSR, and attack east along the beach to link up with the British on Sword. But with the strongpoint on Cap Romain still intact (except perhaps for its two 75-mm guns that were destroyed by tanks), the beach was anything but safe. As Buell watched, the first Marine landing craft ran aground well offshore and then lowered its ramps to allow the men to swim. In Buell's words, they were cut down by machine-gun fire "as though they were a row of wheat sheaves tumbling into the water." Of those who got safely into the water, most drowned, as even the best of swimmers were unable to handle the tidal current. Other Marine landing craft reached the beach, discharging their men in front of the château. There they took shelter under the seawall amid, as their War Diary records, "a jumble of men from other units, including many wounded and dead." They eventually slipped off the beach along the route taken by B and D Companies. Buell spoke briefly to their CO, who was shaken by the loss of half his men. Before heading back to his headquarters, Buell urged Major Forbes of B Company to find tanks, employ them promptly, and "take chances" in his attack on the strongpoint; the regiment's schedule was already falling behind and the beach was not yet secure.

Since coming ashore and moving a short distance inland, the platoons of B Company had withered under the relentless fire from the strongpoint. Lieutenant Richardson's platoon had lost seventeen men to mortars, machine guns, and sniping. Major Forbes learned of their plight when Private H.W. Blakely crossed an open area swept by machine-gun fire "with compete disregard for his own personal safety," with the news. Informed that help was on the way, Blakely sprinted back to Richardson to tell him the news. This heroism earned Blakely the Military Medal. It's hard to determine, now, which tanks arrived first and precisely what was done. The two-pronged assault on the strongpoint was supported by Fort Garry tanks and, by some reports, Churchill AVREs of the British Engineers. It's more likely, however, that the "tanks" with the stubby guns that fought alongside the NSR in clearing St. Aubin were Centaurs of 2 RMAS.

For most of their first hour ashore, the Centaurs provided indirect fire support from their position west of St. Aubin, near the railway line behind la Rive. This job was better suited to the self-propelled (SP) 105-mm guns of the 19th Field Regiment, RCA, which started to land at 0910. The first of 19th RCA to come ashore were the four guns and Sherman tank Observation Post (OP) of D Troop, followed within minutes by C, E, and F Troops for a total of sixteen guns in all. The landing of A Troop was delayed after a mortar bomb landed squarely in one Self-Propelled as the LCT approached, setting fire to two other guns and some vehicles. As a result, A Troop did not land until 1600 and B Troop, whose LCT had propellor troubles, did not get ashore until 1500. But sixteen guns crossed Nan Red between 0910 and 0930, and by 0920 Q Battery reported itself ready to fire. When that happened, the Centaurs were ordered into the village to support the North Shore. Only Centaurs were capable of the high volume of fire the NSR attributed to "AVREs" during the battle at St. Aubin.

The Rue Canet, St. Aubin, late morning on D-Day. B Company infantry take shelter at a roadblock just before the final gun position, which is visible in this shot. The position and its gun — the last *in situ* on this stretch of the D-Day beaches — remains today. IWM

With armoured support, D Company swept through the main portion of the village with comparative ease, but the strongpoint on the promontory of Cap Romain was a much harder nut to crack. B Company could not have done it without the mortar, artillery, tank, and machine-gun fire that became available shortly after 0900. Indeed, the combined-arms assault fairly quickly produced white flags from the main position. But as the NSR infantry moved in, the Germans opened fire again. A renewed combined assault by tanks and infantry resulted in more white flags.

As Captain Bill Harvey of B Company recounted, "the North Shore had had enough of that trickery and went in with bombs, cold steel and shooting . . . and cleaned out the place."

Buell had assigned one hour for capturing the strongpoint, but in the end it took eight to clear it and the town. The strongpoint was an elaborate system of concrete positions linked by tunnels and trenches on the promontory itself, and by tunnels throughout the village. According to Lieutenant McCann, "[t]he position turned out to be far more impregnable than anyone ever imagined and the underground was an engineer's nightmare." The 50-mm gun position on the seawall in the village, which remains in place to this day, had to be taken repeatedly; it was captured eventually by a two-pronged attack down Rue Canet and Rue Gambetta. The attackers worked their way through the village and strongpoint by destroying roadblocks with Centaur fire to allow tanks to get forward to engage the next series of gun positions, then clearing the next obstacles with Centaurs again before leapfrogging the tanks forward. The attack through the streets was also supported by a section of Bren gun carriers from the Support Company and the battalion's anti-tank guns (which landed about 0930). Meanwhile, infantry cleared the buildings, using every tool they had, including anti-tank grenades, occasionally mounted on poles to blast open bricked-up windows and doors. The job was made much worse because the buildings "were joined together by underground passages," according to Captain J.A. Currie of the carrier platoon. It took some time for the NSR to figure out what was going on, but, as Currie recalled, "by persistent fire and rushes 'B' Company got them out and took a lot of prisoners." The only way the final gun on the seawall could be silenced was to blow down a building that obscured it, and then "the anti-tank guns gave it hell." Finally one shot deformed the end of the barrel, and then, as Currie said, "The Jerries poured out with the hands up." The gun emplacement contained seventy spent shell casings: no other German gun along Juno Beach was fought for so long.

The liberation of St. Aubin was watched from windows and doorways by some of the three hundred residents who remained — mostly old men, women, and children. The Canadians had been warned about collaborators offering poisoned food, and Buell professed himself suspicious of any French left in the beach zone. But the mortar platoon was amazed when, as they were setting up their tubes, "old women, teenagers, and everything" poured out of basements, weeping and declaring the Canadians their liberators. Ernie Anderson recalled that wine was offered to the NSR at almost every home, which they declined. "We missed one hell of a party," he wrote later. Anderson was also deeply moved by the efforts of civilians to tend to the wounded and put out fires: "one could not help but admire their courage." With many fluently bilingual New Brunswickers around, communications with the French was not a problem, except perhaps for the battalion's Acadians, whose accent was often incomprehensible to the locals.

Lieutenant McCann's platoon was tasked with clearing out the final diehards in St. Aubin. It took him two hours to search the whole complex. In the end, the NSR captured eighty prisoners in the village and strongpoint and found another fifty enemy dead. This was nearly three times the original intelligence estimate of St. Aubin's garrison, whose *Osttruppen* had fought very well. The NSR War Diary — and subsequent historians — recorded the strongpoint secure at 1115, after three hours of intense fighting. But McCann's platoon did not winkle out the last enemy until 1800 that evening, and they were ordered to "sleep on" the position until the next morning.

With the capture of the strongpoint and village, the battle for the beachhead was over, and the Commandos passed through D Company to start their attack towards Langrune-sur-Mer at 1200. AVREs had cleared gap N.7 above the beach, but the delay in capturing the strongpoint and the storm surge in the Channel prevented engineers from clearing the beach for traffic until the next low tide that evening. Apart from that, Nan Red had gone extremely well.

In fact, the NSR landing went so well that most Canadian historians give it little space in their accounts of D-Day. But there was nothing weak about *Wiederstandneste 27*, as the struggle for the strongpoint proved. What made the difference all along Juno Beach that morning was the determination of the Canadian infantry to fight at close quarters once they got inside the beach defences. That drive carried the Reginas and the Winnipegs into and through the concrete, wire, and guns around Courseulles. And it allowed the Queen's Own to prevail after landing, unintentionally, right in front of the main defences of Bernières, leaving forty men dead below the high-water mark, and yet carry on to complete their assignment.

The North Shore accomplishment was nothing less. A Company, the premier assault company in the whole 3rd Division, cut through the defences at la Rive like a hot knife through butter. The drill for breeching the wire and moving forward worked superbly. Once inside the houses and gardens along the beachfront, A Company could not be stopped. When Captain C.G. Gammon, commander of the Support Company, saw Major Archie McNaughton that morning "He was all smiles." His company was secure on its objectives and ready to move inland, a move that cost them fifty men killed, wounded, and missing. And despite the problems encountered by B Company, it and all the other companies of the NSR moved smartly off the beach, too. The leadership and heroism displayed by Lieutenant Moran in getting his platoon moving when it was trapped against the seawall was noteworthy, but not unique. All along Nan Red, well-trained and motivated men from the North Shore cut their way through the wire or found gaps and moved quickly inland. Sixty years later Arthur Hache's most vivid memory of the actual landing was the urgency to get forward: "Il faut que tu fonces, il faut que tu avances, C'est cela, avance, avance." "Au débarquement," Hache recalled, "quand tu passes au ras des monsieurs, des amis que tu connais et puis qui crient apres toi 'viens m'aider, 'viens m'aider,' et puis t'es pas capable, tu peux pas les aider, il faut que tu continues." Hache remains haunted by the image of a tank crewman on fire, calling for help, as he raced by. But the anguished memories of an aging veteran should not obscure what the younger Arthur Hache and the men of the North Shore understood clearly: their job as assault infantry.

The task of helping the wounded and

Father Myles Hickey, the North Shore's remarkable padre. 2RNBR

removing the dead belonged to others. In the case of the North Shore, this fell to Lieutenant John L. Heaslip and his stretcher bearers of the 22nd Canadian Field Ambulance, the stretcher bearers of the platoons, and to Padre Myles Hickey and Captain J.A. Patterson, the battalion's doctor. Heaslip, Hickey, and Patterson were all decorated for their actions on the beach, as was one of Heaslip's men. "It was a hard job to get the wounded onto stretchers and carry them to the shelter of the wall," Hickey wrote after the war. "I will never forget the courage of the stretcher bearers and first aid men that morning." His courage was no less. D-Day was the start of a charmed existence for Father Hickey, a native of Jacquet River and the parish priest from Newcastle. He gave last rites in combat for the first time to the soldier who was at his side as they stepped together off the LCA; Hickey dragged the fatally wounded young man to shore and anointed him. Hickey spent most of the next two hours pulling the dead and wounded to safety and helping Doc Patterson and the stretcher bearers. "I like to think that a German sniper had me in his telescopic sights," Hickey recalled, "but when he saw by my collar and red cross arm band that I was a chaplain, he stayed his finger." Perhaps so. But shells and mines did not discriminate. At one point Hickey was reported dead when a shell landed amid the three wounded men he had just reached: they all died, he escaped unhurt. Later, while following two stretcher bearers over the wall to retrieve several wounded, everyone ahead of him — the wounded included — died in a huge blast when someone stepped on a mine. Hickey and Major Daughney were blown clear, picked themselves up, and carried on. It seems Father Hickey may have had some help from a higher authority.

The strength of the strongpoint and the tenacity of St. Aubin's defenders, some willing to fight on in ones and twos for the rest of the day, upset the timetable slightly and caused serious casualties on the landing beaches, especially to the Royal Marines. Nan Red was not, as Lieutenant "Bones" McCann anticipated, a "pushover." But in the final analysis, perhaps Nan Red went so well because Buell was right: the North Shore was one of the best battalions in the army.

THE ATTACK ON TAILLEVILLE

By the time the strongpoint was declared cleared at 1115 hours, phase two had already begun: the attack on the village of Tailleville, two and a half kilometres south of St. Aubin across flat, open farmland. This was the start of what Buell planned as a series of company actions: leapfrogging forward, taking Tailleville, the woods south of Tailleville, the radar station at Douvres, and ending up on the brigade objective south of Anguerny — nine kilometres inland — by nightfall. It was a tall order for men already exhausted by several nights without sleep, seasickness, and hours of intense combat. It also proved to be vastly overly ambitious: the NSR never got close to Anguerny on D-Day.

When Buell ordered C Company up the road to Tailleville shortly before noon there was no reason to believe the plan could not be met. All the elements he needed were in place, including the various parts of his own battalion, plus tank and artillery support. Away to the west, on the flat slope rising from Bernières, other elements of the 8th Brigade, including the Chaudières, were now moving south as well, while the 3rd Division's reserve Brigade, the 9th, had begun to land at Bernières. Further west, and well out of sight amid the smoke of battle, the 7th Brigade was moving up either side of the Seulles River valley against only scattered resistance. Things were going well.

And so while D Company moved to the southeast of St. Aubin to secure the flank of the beachhead, C Company advanced toward

Tailleville. Major Ralph Daughney, originally from Fredericton but of late the mill manager at Nelson on the Miramichi, was described by Sergeant Albanie Drapeau as a man who "didn't fear anything." Certainly, fear did not keep Daughney from reconnoitering the ground on a bicycle before the attack started. For the advance on Tailleville, he deployed two platoons up, one in reserve, and was supported by Fort Garry tanks and the NSR mortar platoon led by Drapeau. A Forward Observation Officer (FOO) from 19th Field was assigned to provide artillery support. The Bren carrier platoon covered the flanks and swung around to the west side of Tailleville to cut off any escaping enemy. Buell and the battalion HQ followed close behind C Company. Meanwhile, A Company followed behind C by five hundred yards and was tasked with sweeping around the village and occupying the woods behind.

As soon as C Company moved south of St. Aubin, German mortar bombs began landing; but these did nothing to stop the attack. "The tanks gave us good support," Captain LeBlanc remembered, "so we kept slowly moving ahead." When Major Daughney wanted 19th RCA to open fire on the village, the FOO could not be found, and it took some time before the 105-mm guns, still in position at la Rive, poured fire into Tailleville. So, too, did the heavy mortars of the Cameron Highlanders of Ottawa. Eventually, as C Company closed within a few hundred metres of the village, it came under intense machine-gun fire and the attack slowed.

From the north, Tailleville looks like a medieval fortress, with a long ten-foot-high stone wall running east-west across the front for several hundred yards. By June 1944, it was loopholed for rifles and machine guns and supported along its seaward face by a series of concrete pillboxes. Trenches and some outer works ran into the field in front. The road from St. Aubin runs to the east end of the wall, and across the road there was — and still is — a small copse of trees. It was from there that the heaviest machine-gun fire came.

As small-arms fire drove C Company to ground, Daughney ordered his mortars to silence the guns in the small copse. "[Captain] LeBlanc showed me the exact clump of trees he wanted fire brought down on,"

Major John A. McNaughton, A Company's commander on D-Day and the most senior member of the regiment killed that day. 2RNBR

Sergeant Drapeau recalled. "Luckily I made a quick correction in degrees and the first ranging rounds fell exactly where he wanted them." In fact, Drapeau was noted for his skill in getting a hit the first time, and it paid off in the attack on Tailleville. With the machine guns in the copse of trees silenced and Canadian fire raining down on the village, Captain LeBlanc brigaded the company mortars to provide a fire support base, and the leading platoons of C Company rushed the entrance to the château and surged around the village.

Meanwhile, Buell arrived at the entrance to the village, having crawled on his belly for a hundred yards to avoid enemy fire. There, where the road from St. Aubin and the château wall meet, Major Daughney reported Tailleville secure. Buell doubted it. He ordered C Company to "clear the village again and repeat this operation until the fire on the beach had ceased, even if he had to do it four or five times." Daughney, none too happy about his orders, went back to work. Meanwhile, A Company began to sweep around Tailleville on its way to the forest further south. One small copse of trees on the eastern side was assigned to Fred Moar's platoon. They raced across the open fields, "rifles at the high port," and arrived without casualties. The rest of A Company appears to have passed west of the village. In the centre, Buell "gathered Major McNaughton and his company headquarters

The ambush of A Company headquarters, Tailleville: 1, the road from St. Aubin taken by Buell, McNaughton and their group; 2, the Cassigneul farm; 3, where McNaughton, and several others died; 4, where Buell and Bill Savage sheltered; 5, route of the tank that extracted Buell; 6, château; 7, site of the barn (which burned on June 6) from which the fatal machine-gun burst came. Monsieur Cassigneul was killed on D-Day by a Canadian grenade, one of three civilians to die in Tailleville in the fighting. M. Cassigneul

party and told him we would move through the village now that it had been cleared." The reserve platoon of A Company followed them down the road into the village.

Having told Major Daughney that Tailleville was not clear, Buell ought to have heeded his own warning. Tailleville was the headquarters of the 2nd battalion of the German 736th Regiment. It was a warren of prepared defences and underground structures held by a company of infantry. If C Company had indeed passed through, the Germans had simply let them slip past. "The village was a strongpoint," Sergeant Drapeau said, "and the fighting went on all afternoon as the whole garrison was dug in underground, first aid posts, garages, stables [with horses and other livestock in them], everything, and tunnels to every place." Buell discovered this shortly after he, McNaughton, and their headquarters parties set off on the road through the village.

From the entrance to the château the road runs south along the high stone wall of a barn belonging to the Cassigneul farm, then makes a sharp ninety-degree turn to the west following the shape of the barn and runs in front of the main farm entrance. This area formed, as it does today, a small open space enclosed by stone walls and buildings. In front of the farm entrance, the road makes another ninety-degree turn to the south and passes into the village. Buell and McNaughton led the two headquarters parties down the road and around the first sharp corner into the open stretch in front of the farm entrance. Immediately behind McNaughton, and attached to him by a wire and headset, was his company signaller, Bill Savage, followed by Jack Kingston, the signals sergeant, Harold Daley of the intelligence section, Art Strang, the major's Batman, Hech Archer and Billy Adair, both stretcher bearers, and trailing behind them all portions of the reserve platoon. It proved to be a faulty and fatal deployment.

Savage recalls that the HQ group had nearly reached the farm entrance when they saw three Germans hitching a horse. Everyone but Savage knelt to start firing as the Germans quickly scattered. In an instant a machine gun sited in the open loft door of a barn overlooking the area from the west (it has since been replaced by a house) opened fire. According the Buell's account, at this stage they thought the fire was coming from ground level, so they threw some smoke grenades and Buell assumed that everyone would wait for the cloud to build before they moved again. Smoke grenades made a little "pop" when the charge went off, and it took a few seconds for the cloud to build and become a useful cover. According to Buell, Archie McNaughton, his runner, and his two signallers all moved when they heard the pop. The next burst of fire killed McNaughton, Daley, and Strang, and fatally wounded Archer and Adair. Kingston had two fingers shot off his right hand, and one bullet struck Savage in the chest. With McNaughton now lying dead on the earphone cable attached to the radio, Savage was unable to escape as other machine guns began to rake the road. When supporting troops started to return fire, Buell grabbed Savage and dragged him through the farm gate and under the shelter of a slate roof.

Buell and Savage were now trapped in the courtyard of the Cassigneul farm. German machine gunners chipped away at the stone sheltering the NSR's commanding officer, as hand grenades exploded above, sending a shower of slate to the ground. Buell dressed Savage's wound, returned fire, and threw all of his own and the signaller's six grenades. After several agonizing minutes, a Fort Garry tank smashed its way through a barn at the north end of the farm compound and moved up to shelter Buell, just as another tank poked its gun around the corner of the road into the scene of the battle. Buell told Savage to lay still until help came and retreated through the farm compound with the tank.

Buell recounted later that "immediately after this, a platoon of C Company moved through this area from a different direction, and managed to wipe out both the grenade thrower and the men in the machine-gun post." But for Bill Savage, lying alone in his own blood in a Normandy farmyard while battle swirled around him, the wait seemed an eternity. At one point, a large black Alsatian dog approached, and Savage had premonitions of being eaten alive. But the dog sniffed and then trotted happily away. Savage was listed among the dead, but he was eventually evacuated to the beach and received a life-saving transfusion around 1800. Archie McNaughton, the over-age farmer from Black River and Great War veteran who desperately wanted to lead his men into battle, was not so fortunate: only Savage and Kingston survived from A Company's HQ.

The battle for Tailleville lasted for about five hours. Every time the NSR swept through the village, the Germans popped up again. The Canadians learned later that Tailleville was connected through a network of tunnels to St. Aubin, Bernières, Douvres, the forest south of the village, and probably the radar station. It was like St. Aubin all over again. The last message from the headquarters of the German 2nd battalion, 736th Regiment, at Tailleville was transmitted around 1500: "Hand-to-hand fighting in the command post. We are hemmed into a closely confined area, but are still holding out." All of the available Fort Garry tanks got involved in the fighting. Gradually, in ones or twos and small groups, the German defenders surrendered. Many were encouraged to do so when Captain LeBlanc grabbed a flame thrower and worked his way through a maze of tunnels. Flame is a dreadful weapon and few men are foolhardy enough to resist when it is applied at close quarters. Tailleville proved no exception.

Nonetheless, Daughney's men cleared the village six times before they were certain that the last German had been flushed out. When Father Hickey saw the first group of prisoners, they were trembling: "You could see they thought we were going to shoot them." Such a fate might well have been better, according to Hickey, than "the awful barrage of words and tongue lashing they got from Captain [B.S.A.] McElwaine." Tailleville was declared secure at 2100 hours, at a cost of fourteen Canadians — most from the NSR — and an untold number of Germans: only fifty of the strongpoint's estimated one hundred plus garrison were captured.

"The strongpoint at St. Aubin and the defence put up at Tailleville had slowed up my plan until it was badly behind schedule," Buell reflected. Nonetheless, by about 1600 hours, the NSR began to sort itself out for the next phase: the attack on the radar station. In fact, Lieutenant Moar's

platoon had probed the outer edges of the northern section of the station in the early stages of the battle. Moar returned pessimistic about any easy success. He carried that news to Buell when he was recalled following McNaughton's death to assume duty as A Company's second in command. Meanwhile, the first tanks of the Garrys nudged their way over the crown of the low rise that separated Tailleville from the radar station, only to be quickly knocked out. This was a portend.

According to the plan, A Company was to secure the forested area south of Tailleville, allowing D Company to use it as a start line for the attack on the radar station. While Buell was preparing to execute this plan, 8th Brigade ordered him to stop and consolidate on Tailleville. The reason for this halt is usually attributed to the prolonged struggle the NSR had already endured. Indeed, one recent British historian has claimed that the "delay imposed on the 3rd Canadian Division by II/736 Grenadiers at Tailleville contributed significantly to their failure to reach their objective on the Caen-Bayeux road on D Day." This goes too far. The decision to hold at Tailleville probably had more to do with the open left flank of the 3rd Canadian Division and the German armoured attack that struck toward the sea in the late afternoon into the gap between Juno and Sword Beaches.

Indeed, the failure to link up the 3rd Canadian and 3rd British Divisions' beaches on D-Day had a major impact on the NSR and subsequent Allied operations around Caen. German beach defenders between St. Aubin and the British landings at Sword fought on, in some cases, until 8 June. British 8th Brigade, which might have established contact with the Canadians on D-Day, was drawn into the ongoing beachhead battle, and the much weakened 48 RM Commando found the going hard. Meanwhile, the leading elements of the 21st Panzer Division probed the gap in the afternoon of June 6, and, at about the time Buell was ordered to consolidate at Tailleville, forty German tanks attacked the western flank of 3rd British Division. The 21st Panzer Division claimed that some of their tanks actually reached the sea at Lion-sur-Mer. Had they turned west instead they would have crashed into the North Shore Regiment. There was, then, good reason in the late afternoon to hold at Tailleville.

It is also true that the North Shore still had plenty to do in Tailleville and it would need some time to consolidate their position for the night. As Buell concluded, "We had had a fairly rugged day." B Company was ordered to dig in south of St. Aubin; D Company secured the eastern flank of Tailleville facing the radar station; A guarded the southern edge of the village; and C was kept in the centre as a reserve. As much as possible the existing German defences were used, shifting wire and firing position to suit the new requirements. By 2200, the NSR were snug in its position. Through the night the men watched warily to the south and east for signs of the enemy, marched prisoners back to the beach, heated a bit of food, counted their losses, and distributed ammunition and orders for the next day.

By the end of June 6, 1944, the North Shore Regiment had gone only halfway to their objectives, but it had broken Hitler's Atlantic Wall, fought its way through the strongest secondary position on Juno Beach, and secured the eastern flank of the Canadian landings. The men's training and preparation had served them well. The men of the North Shore could take pride in their accomplishment — and a few moments to reflect on the cost. Securing their portion of the D-Day beachhead had cost the regiment from northern New Brunswick thirty-three dead and ninety-one wounded.

The Douvres radar station, early 1944. The Tailleville forest is in the bottom of the photo, just below the northern section of the station — the part the North Shore probed on June 6-7. LCMSDS

Chapter Four

Securing the Beachhead

The Canadian assault on Juno Beach was the most successful of the Allied landings on D-Day. By nightfall, the 3rd Canadian Division was on its interim objective eight kilometres inland (code-named ELM), with some formations well beyond. Early the next afternoon, the 7th Brigade established itself astride the Caen-Bayeux highway at Bretteville-l'Orgueilleuse and Putot, becoming the first Allied formation to capture its ultimate D-Day objective. The 9th Brigade was not so fortunate. As it advanced on D+1 towards its final objective of Carpiquet airfield west of Caen, the vanguard was ambushed by two battalions and about forty tanks from the 12th SS Panzer Division (Hitler Youth). British 3rd Division advancing on the Canadians' left was struck at the same time. This was just the first of a wave of counter-attacks by three German Panzer divisions that broke against the Anglo-Canadian defences over the next four days. By June 11, the 3rd Canadian Division was a spent force. As the reserve brigade, the 8th played no direct role in blunting these assaults. Its job through the rest of June was to hold the line. For the men of the North Shore, that meant almost four weeks of continuous contact with the enemy.

As with all the other Allied troops who landed on D-Day, the NSR's first night ashore was anything but restful. Sporadic fighting went on everywhere as patrols clashed, isolated German garrisons attempted to escape, officers tried to locate their units, and supply columns got lost. Amid this confusion, virtually all of the 285 prisoners captured by the NSR on D-Day escaped. At Tailleville the firing went on throughout the short hours of a Normandy summer night. During those few hours of darkness, the regiment was bombed by the German air force, and mortared and sniped at, while a steady stream of parachute flares and anti-aircraft tracers lit up the sky. Morning brought relief only from the pyrotechnics, as the grim business of war continued in earnest. As the day brightened, Padre Hickey and others buried the dead who still lay all around from the previous day's fighting, and Lieutenant-Colonel Buell mustered the battalion for the unfinished business from D-Day: the attack on the radar station at Douvres. In the event, the North Shore was the only Canadian battalion still fully engaged in combat in the beach zone throughout D+1.

Buell must have been anxious about the prospect of tackling the radar station on June 7, for the twenty-five-acre radar complex was a formidable position: it was the largest radar station in lower Normandy. The northern section of the station, which Lieutenant Moar's platoon had probed on the afternoon of D-Day, housed a huge long-range early warning radar with a massive antenna protected by three 20-mm anti-aircraft guns, concrete positions, trenches, and belts of wire. The main site, across the road to the south, was four times bigger and held the two medium-range and two short-range radars used to direct night fighters. By the end of D-Day, the antennas and the surface of the station were in utter ruins from hours of pounding by warships and aircraft. What was not seriously damaged were the thirty concrete defensive works, minefields, anti-tank ditch, extensive wire, and massive, five-story-deep steel-reinforced underground headquarters structure. Apart from the radar equipment, these emplacements held dual-purpose anti-aircraft and ground defence 20-mm and twin machine guns, heavy mortars, five 50-mm anti-tank guns, and at least one 75-mm field howitzer, all encased in concrete. Despite this formidable arsenal, Allied intelligence estimated that the station's garrison, 8 Company of Luftwaffe Regiment No. 53, would have "no stomach for a fight" after the bombardment on

D-Day. They were, of course, quite wrong. Indeed, by D+1 the garrison had been reinforced by the remnants of the 716th Division and numbered at least 230 men, and possibly more.

Buell's orders at the end of D-Day were to contain the station and take it on D+1. Before he could attack, the North Shore had to clear the start line along the woods south of Tailleville. And so, at 0700 on June 7, a much depleted A Company, now at three-quarters strength under its new acting commanding officer, Captain J.L. Belliveau, began securing the woods. Once this was complete, C and D Companies would pass through and set up for D Company's attack on the radar station. In the end, things never got that far.

The forested area south of Tailleville covered about thirty acres, and A Company found it filled with Germans and "honeycombed with trenches." It was, in reality, the headquarters for German artillery in the area. Unable to use artillery support because of the tree cover, Belliveau's men found clearing the woods very slow going. As the morning wore on, Buell grew impatient and sent his intelligence officer, Captain Blake Oulton, forward to see what the problem was. "It was slow work," Oulton recounted later, "with so many trenches and prepared positions to be ferreted out." Eventually, Buell undertook his own reconnaissance. Jumping into Major Bill Bray's tank, and screened by a troop and a half of other Fort Garry Shermans, Buell was driven to the southern end — "the German end," in Buell's words — of the woods. There Buell and Bray dismounted to get their first real look at the radar station. "To my amazement," Buell said, "there seemed to be a steady stream of [German] troops moving from Douvres-la-Délivrande into the radar station." It seems that as the British 3rd Division closed the gap between themselves and the Canadians, many Germans still left along the coast sought refuge in the radar station.

Buell also found many of the enemy still in the wooded area, so he ordered C Company to join the fighting alongside A. If all this was not enough, the battalion once again came under sniper fire in Tailleville. The North Shore's strength was being rapidly dissipated.

One platoon of B Company was still in St. Aubin and was not retrieved until 2100 hours that night, while the rest of that company formed the battalion reserve. D was slated for the attack on the radar station, and A and C were mired in the Tailleville forest. Just how many Germans caused all this trouble remains unclear: the NSR captured only a handful. It is generally accepted that most fled to the west and were corralled by other Canadian troops around Basly. Meanwhile, the 105-mm field guns of the 19th RCA fired on the radar station to keep it busy, as did the Cameron Highlanders of Ottawa's heavy machine guns and mortars that were still attached to the NSR.

It was not until 1600 hours that the forested area was clear enough for Buell to start reorienting his battalion for the attack on the radar station. Major Anderson's D Company would lead the assault on the left, but his men would now be joined by Major Daughney's C Company on the right, in a two-company assault. When the two majors came forward with Buell to get their first glimpse of the station, they were, in his words, "much impressed by the size and strength" of it. No doubt. When the commander of 19th RCA came forward to discuss artillery support for the attack, he could offer them nothing to allay their concerns. The leading elements of the 9th Brigade, making the last dash to their objective at Carpiquet, and British forces to their left had been attacked several hours earlier by the 12th SS Panzer Division (Hitler Youth). Intense mortar and machine-gun fire from the radar station had already delayed artillery support for the struggling 9th Brigade by forcing 14th RCA from its gun positions near Basly. The only big guns available, the nine 6-inch guns of the cruiser HMS *Belfast* (the equivalent of a medium artillery battery), were dedicated to stopping the Hitler Youth. The NSR would have to make do with the twenty 105-mm guns of the 19th, its own mortars and a few 4-inch mortars from the Camerons. Most had already seen the affect this was having on the steel-reinforced concrete of the radar station's positions. In Padre Hickey's words, firing 105-mm shells at the station "was like blowing soap bubbles against Gibraltar."

If this was not enough to give Buell pause, the fate of C Company and a Churchill AVRE probably was. As the NSR prepared for the attack, a British engineer arrived and enquired of Major Forbes what the problem was. When told, the Englishman said "Well, well, we'll soon fix that!" and then turned and shouted "Bring up the Petard!" In due course, along came a Churchill AVRE, its petard mortar in the turret loaded with a huge shaped charge explosive that was designed to destroy concrete emplacements. Despite the warnings of Forbes and others, the British major jumped in the vehicle and it rumbled towards the radar station. Within seconds the Churchill was completely destroyed in a powerful explosion. After that "Bring up the Petard!" became a cliché in the NSR. Meanwhile, when C Company moved to the start line it came under intense fire from the radar station and had to retreat into the woods.

With that Buell decided the radar station was well beyond the capabilities of his battalion, although he hesitated slightly when the rest of the squadron of Churchill AVREs arrived. After consultation with brigade headquarters, however, the NSR were ordered to move west of the wooded area at 1800 and join the rest of the brigade in their positions around Anguerny. The enormous challenge of taking the radar station with a weak battalion and little fire support may well account for Buell's caution on June 7. It is clear that he was not prepared to commit the NSR to heavy losses taking the woods, nor could he afford to if he had any hope of tackling the station. In the event, the NSR suffered only eighteen casualties on D+1, and the job of tackling the radar station passed to the newly arrived 51st Highland Division.

Now came the final indignity of a frustrating day. Before the NSR could move off from its newly won positions in the Tailleville woods, it was attacked by the British Army's 5th Battalion Black Watch and its supporting tanks. In fact, the battalion was still in the forest when, as Lieutenant W.K. Dickie of D Company recalled, it "immediately came under heavy fire from machine guns and tanks" to its rear. Major Anderson discovered the problem when most of D Company simply went to ground, while his forward platoon and C Company bolted south over open ground. Anderson ran out and stopped the tank fire, but the Black Watch "fought" their way through the woods despite his pleas. "I fully expected to find few

Writing home. Anguerny, June 8, 1944. LAC PA-132800

of our men alive." Anderson said. But casualties were light, just several wounded. The Black Watch desperately wanted to come to grips with the enemy and had little time for anyone in their way. Nor were they interested in the information that Buell and his officers could provide.

While the North Shore moved off towards Anguerny, Blake Oulton and several others stayed on to watch the British attack on the radar station. It opened with three Churchill AVREs moving forward, all of which were destroyed in quick succession. As Oulton commented, "The Black Watch never moved out of the woods to the positions we had taken." The Highlanders soon passed the station on to the 4th Special Service

Brigade of the Royal Marines, who took another ten days to capture it. In the meantime, the radar station at Douvres was a thorn in the side of the Anglo-Canadian beachhead, and with its secure communications (including buried telephone cables) and excellent observation kept the Germans informed of events behind the Allied lines. It is tantalizing to think what might have been accomplished had the NSR been able to take the position quickly on D-Day.

By late in the day on June 7, the NSR were reunited with their brigade in the fortress position around Anguerny. The rest of 8th Brigade had spent the day cleaning up pockets of resistance and German stragglers behind the front and securing the divisional reserve line. The North Shore remained around Anguerny for the next three days, and it was here that the battalion was restored to nearly full strength. Lieutenant "Bones" McCann and his platoon rejoined the battalion from St. Aubin after a harrowing nighttime trip that accidentally led them to the perimeter of the radar station. The first batch of reinforcements, three junior officers and eleven men, also stumbled in on the eighth. They had landed on D-Day on the other side of Courseulles-sur-Mer and were detained briefly by the Chaudières as reinforcements.

At 0100 hours the next day, a further four officers and sixty-nine men arrived. They, too, had landed on D-Day with much difficulty. When their LCT ran aground and could not be moved, the men elected to wade to the beach through water that was well over many of their heads. Undeterred and heavily burdened by their equipment, a few of those too short to keep their heads above water used their rifles as a breathing tube and walked ashore submerged. Three drowned in the process. It took them most of two days to find the battalion, but the arrival of nearly one hundred men and some officers on the eighth did much to restore the NSR's fighting strength. The battalion's quartermaster, Sergeant E.J. Russell, and some of its supporting trucks and supplies also caught up with the NSR at Anguerny. Like the others, they too had a terrible time just getting ashore. Unable to land on the sixth because of congestion at Bernières, they

Foot care, a constant preoccupation for infantry. Anguerny, June 8, 1944.

came ashore the next day, but their Landing Ship, Tank — a huge vessel of 5,000 tons with two decks and giant bow doors that opened like a clamshell — ran aground three hundred metres offshore. The first vehicle to drive out simply dropped off the ramp and got stuck nose first on the bottom. It had to be winched out with a cable. The larger trucks, including those of the NSR, fared better, and Russell lost only one. They assembled at their concentration point on the seventh and moved forward to the NSR positions at Anguerny the next day. Although the North

Shore's fighting echelon was now largely complete, the rest of the battalion's support and administrative elements did not land until late June.

While the North Shore was dug in around Anguerny, the battle with the 12th SS raged along the 7th and 9th Brigade fronts south of them. Only once, on the night of June 8/9, did elements of the Hitler Youth — in the early days mistaken by most Canadians for paratroops because of their camouflage uniforms — reach the NSR position. On that black night, as Lieutenant McCann recalled, "a handful of Jerry paratroopers, youngsters not more than seventeen years old" stumbled onto B Company. What alarmed the North Shore most was that all the young Nazis seemed to be carrying Canadian service revolvers — evidence, had they known it, of the over-running of two companies of The North Nova Scotia Highlanders at Authie the day before. In a short time, the North Shore men would have cause to fear and loath those teenagers in the mottled camouflage suits.

As the battle west of Caen settled down into a struggle for position, the 8th Brigade was drawn into the gap between the two front-line brigades that ran along the Mue River. On June 9, the NSR slipped forward slightly to occupy positions vacated by the QOR. Late on the tenth, the warning came to be ready to move. At 0730 the next day, on a clear but cool morning, the North Shore shifted their position to Cairon, going into the line to the right of the 9th Brigade. The early morning march through the fresh Normandy countryside left a lasting impression on Padre Hickey, and probably on many of the deeply religious Catholics of the NSR who took comfort in the "calvaries at the crossroads that seemed to come to life in the breaking dawn." The more literate among them would no doubt have seen the symbolism in the larks that darted amid the trees along the roadside and the blood-red poppies that lined their route.

The NSR settled into Cairon, sent out patrols, and started drawing fire from the enemy. Meanwhile, the rest of 8th Brigade was employed in limited attacks. The Chaudières and 46 RM Commando, supported by tanks, wrestled the Hitler Youth for the village of

Rots in the wooded valley of the Mue River. Its capture closed the gap between the 9th Brigade in the east and the 7th Brigade in the west. The QOR were temporarily attached to the 7th Brigade. On June 11, they were ordered to push the Canadian line south of Bretteville and Putot to the high ground around the village of le Mesnil-Patry. This attack was, in the words of Queen's Own history, an operation "conceived in sin and born in inequity."

The attack on le Mesnil-Patry was mounted in haste, but it was not without purpose. By D+4 there was still a gap in the German front lines south of Bayeux, and the British planned to push their 7th Armoured Division through it. British 50th Division, to the right of the Canadians, was attacking in support of this operation and a concerted push south of Putot/Bretteville would help them. So D Company of the QOR was ordered to join up with B Squadron of the 1st Hussars from London, Ontario, and attack across two kilometres of open ground to le Mesnil-Patry. This was the first phase of a two-stage operation towards Cristot. Despite the protests of their officers, the battle group was given no time to reconnoiter the area, discuss the situation with the troops in the forward positions or to tee-up fire support. Nor had the QOR ever trained or operated with the 1st Hussars. Regardless of all this, at 1400 D Company and B Squadron of the 1st Hussars drove through the 7th Brigade lines at Norrey without ever stopping — and into the waiting guns of a full battalion of the 12th SS and their supporting tanks. The result was a slaughter. Up to that point, D Company had suffered only thirteen casualties. Of the 105 men who rode into battle on June 11 at le Mesnil-Patry, ninety-six were killed, wounded, or captured. Only nine escaped uninjured. B Squadron of the 1st Hussars was virtually wiped out, suffering eighty men killed or wounded. Phase two never got started. The NSR was never part of the fiasco at le Mesnil-Patry, but it later got the unenviable duty of clearing the battlefield.

For five days, the North Shore held the line near Cairon and Lasson, patrolling, sniping, digging, and being shelled. At Cairon the Germans had excellent observation over the NSR's positions: consequently, no matter where they moved, the shells found them. Several men were killed when shells burst in tree tops, sending the blast down into their trenches.

The exposed position at Cairon produced a steady drain of casualties: two killed on the tenth, four on the eleventh plus eight injured, and three more dead on the twelfth. One of those killed at Cairon was Corporal Howie Aubie of the carrier platoon, the composer of the regiment's unofficial march, "The Old North Shore." When Captain Belliveau, the acting commander of A Company, was wounded, Major Anderson was shifted from D Company to command A, while Captain Clint Gammon was promoted and took over D Company.

The move to Lasson-Rosel in the Mue valley brought relief from the constant shelling, although Major Daughney narrowly escaped death on a patrol when a bullet penetrated his helmet and creased his forehead. Others were killed on patrols or died when the German air force again bombed them. But the greatest moment of panic came when A Company reported a tank assault on the morning of the fifteenth. The warning rebounded throughout the whole brigade and everyone — even the cooks — stood to. The tension only eased when the brigade discovered that A Company was actually in reserve, and on further examination the tanks turned out to be a heard of cows, in Will Bird's words, "ambling down a pasture trail."

The North Shore were ordered forward to le Mesnil-Patry late on the seventeenth. Major G.E. Lockwood, the second in command, and Lieutenant Oulton, the intelligence officer, had already done a reconnaissance, arranging the takeover from The Royal Winnipeg Rifles, who had just occupied the position. "Dark came and we started off," Father Hickey wrote in his memoir, "through Bray and Bretteville-l'Orgueilleuses (Bretteville The Proud), now a heap of ruins with only a gaunt shell-pierced church tower left to tell you of its former pride. You could smell death in the air; and, when the moon came up, you could see dead bodies along the roadside." It only got worse. "On crossing the rail at Putot-en-Bessin we were assailed by the most offensive stench of the dead," Oulton remembered. "On that battlefield along with the dead soldiers of opposing armies there were scattered the carcasses of many cattle and horses

lying bloated in the hot sun. German and Canadian tanks were all about, knocked out hulks. There were sixteen Sherman tanks lying almost in line abreast before the village where they had been shot up." It was a scene from hell, and some of the Winnipegs "were quite jittery" when the NSR arrived just before dawn.

They had every reason to be jittery. The Canadians were still facing the fanatical Hitler Youth of the 12th SS, who by this stage had shot nearly 150 Canadian prisoners, many of them from the RWR. When Fred Moar arrived at le Mesnil-Patry, he saw a line of dead officers from the QOR assembled along the road as if for medical treatment. Each one had a bullet through the head. "I knew them all," he recalls with profound sadness. Burial parties were organized by Lieutenant Bernard McElwaine and Sergeant Mike Sullivan of the pioneer platoon. All after-noon and early evening on the seventeenth, narrow graves were dug, caps removed, and silence observed as Father Hickey said a few words over small groups of bodies. An armoured bulldozer was brought up from the beach to scrape a long trench and push as many of the animal carcasses as possible into it. It took days for the smell to subside — or for the men to become accustomed to it — and in the meantime some were so ill they had to be evacuated temporarily.

Buell deployed three companies along the southern edge of the vil-lage: A on the left, D in the centre, and C on the right, with B in reserve and battalion HQ tucked safely into a stone barn on the north side. For the next ten days, le Mesnil-Patry was home to the NSR. And although it was well forward, under fire, and subject to constant probing by German patrols, the village had its compensations. The most important of these was food. As Father Hickey recalled, "Only one little animal was safe, the sheep." After years of living on mutton in Britain, the men wanted noth-ing to do with sheep. But le Mesnil-Patry abounded in cattle, chickens, and ducks — and horses if your taste ran to that. As Hickey observed, no one from the NSR "would stoop to mutton, with steaks and pork chops walking around." Even after the army issued a strict order prohibiting living off the land, le Mesnil-Patry, with its minefields and snipers, pro-duced a bounty. Indeed, cattle had a habit of blowing up on German minefields and revealing their presence, and for that reason the Germans tried to shoot them. Either way, there was a lot of beef available. The day the order came down to restrict themselves to army rations, June 21, 1944, Lieutenant McElwaine dined on roast duck and pig liver, and two days later, enjoyed twenty-five-year-old cognac and steak for breakfast. Milk and eggs simply had to be collected. When Major Gammon was invited to dine with Lieutenant E.T. Gorman's platoon one evening, he arrived to find a barn door covered with a cloth and stacked high with steak, potatoes, carrots, pickles, and chow. Music played in the background from a scrounged gramophone. The only thing that marred the evening was a spent tank round that came through the roof and knocked down a beam while they were having tea.

During its stay in le Mesnil-Patry, the NSR was barely five hundred yards from the German positions. They exchanged fire routinely and their patrols fought one another. Fred Moar got fed up with spending all day in his slit trench and rolled out onto the grass for a bit of sunlight; but one well-placed shot ripping over his head drove him back into the ground. When Captain Phillip Oland of Saint John arrived as a new FOO from the 12th RCA, his first shot wounded or killed four Germans — they were seen to fall and were carried away. In response, the Germans knocked the roof off Oland's observation post, wounding two of his men. Generally, artillery or mortar fire drew retaliation on the infantry positions opposite. Lieutenant-Colonel Freddie Clifford, commanding officer of the 13th RCA, found that the best way to stop the enemy artillery from firing was to fire at their infantry and get them to tell their own people to stop. Oland learned this at le Mesnil-Patry from the NSR, who preferred it if the big guns remained silent while it was in the line.

The really dangerous work was done on patrols, and by all accounts the men of the North Shore were good at this very risky job. "Unless one has led night patrols in a weird and utterly strange no man's land," according to Lieutenant C.F. Richardson, "the feelings are hard to describe." On the night of the nineteenth, Richardson led a patrol that slithered along

Six 3-inch mortars, like the one seen here being fired in training by an unidentified 3rd Division unit just prior to D-Day, gave the infantry battalion its own integral fire support. The ten-pound bomb had a range of 1,600 yards. LAC

a tank track in the wheat field separating the two sides. When a German patrol appeared on the other track going the opposite way, Richardson and his men went dead still and let them pass. On that patrol the only serious incident occurred while trying to get back into the NSR position. The sentry refused to accept their password and threw a grenade which bounced off Richardson before exploding. One man was wounded and

Richardson's "beret and tunic were shredded," but he was not hurt. According to Will Bird, Lieutenant Paul McCann had "an uncanny knack of finding his way about" while on patrol, and Blake Oulton noted McCann's "coolness in going out and coming back off patrols," seldom armed with anything more than two hand grenades.

The rate and intensity of patrols increased starting June 20 in anticipation of a major British offensive, Operation EPSOM, designed to sweep west of Caen and seize the high ground of Hill 112 across the Odon River. On that day Lieutenant-Colonel Buell escorted a British brigadier around the battalion area, and the next day officers of the British 15th Scottish Division arrived to see the ground over which they would attack. The activity was noticed by the Germans, who responded with increased shelling, prompting the commander of the British attacking corps, General R.A. O'Connor, to write on the twenty-fifth to thank 3rd Canadian Division for its help and to apologize for any casualties caused.

Starting on the twenty-fourth, the NSR and the rest of 8th Brigade began a series of fighting patrols to unsettle the Germans, deny them freedom of movement, and screen the deployment of the 15th Division behind the brigade. The patrol orders for the night of June 24/25 required that one platoon — over thirty men — commanded by an officer be sent out. Its task was to capture enemy prisoners so that the formation opposite could be identified, kill "as many of the enemy as possible," pinpoint "any enemy strong pts [points] that can be subsequently engaged by arty [artillery], 4.2" mortar, M.M.G.s [medium machine guns] or bn [battalion] weapons," and finally generally harass the enemy. Two fighting patrols went out that night, one platoon led by McCann that brought back information and another led by Lieutenant R.V. Wilby that found a large German working party and called down artillery fire on it. On the next day, the twenty-fifth, the British 49th Division on the NSR right began a local attack, and another fighting patrol went out that night.

Finally, at 0719 on the morning of June 26, the leading elements of the 15th Scottish Division passed through the North

Shore to launch Operation EPSOM. Ten minutes later, eight hundred guns of the 2nd British Army opened fire, the earth trembled, and, barely two hundred yards ahead of the NSR forward companies, the supporting barrage fell. The battalion's War Diary described it as "the greatest artillery barrage yet to be laid down" in Normandy. Some rounds fell short, and at least one NSR soldier was killed. "The shells seemed to come right at us for about ten minutes," said Clint Gammon, "and as soon as the barrage lifted the attackers went through us with their tanks on the flank. It was all over in an hour. The Germans were either killed or retreated." The anticipated German counter-barrage did not arrive until 1120. Until then, Father Hickey and Doc Patterson went forward to help with the British wounded and returned when shells began to land amid their own men. Fortunately only a few were wounded. Later, Buell sent some of his men to have a look at the German positions. They found the bunkers piled with dead. "The slaughter had been terrible," Gammon recalled. The NSR did find one wounded German with no fight left in him. Gammon gave him a cigarette and sent him back to the NSR lines in his jeep.

Operation EPSOM, launched by British VIIIth Corps, lasted from June 26 until June 30. It gained a foothold across the Odon River and briefly held the heights at Hill 112 overlooking Caen. But savage counterattacks by three Panzer divisions and elements of three others stalled the attack at great cost: 4,020 British soldiers killed, wounded, or missing in three days of brutal fighting. The only saving grace of the battle was the destruction of the German counter-attack launched on the EPSOM salient by 2nd SS Panzer Corps, the force the Germans had been assembling for their own attack. More importantly for the NSR, as the Canadians slipped forward to cover the flank of the advancing British, it was now facing Caen: the ultimate D-Day objective of 2nd British Army, just a few short kilometres away across a flat plain.

Long before the EPSOM battle collapsed on the barren and fire-swept slopes of Hill 112, the North Shore was heading into reserve. They had been at le Mesnil-Patry for ten days and suffered two dead and thirteen wounded. But during their twenty-two days in the line, the new men had been integrated and the battalion had learned a great deal about war.

As Will Bird observed, "Every platoon had a large crop of new faces, and promotions had placed stripes on many old hands who had had full training." More importantly, a month of combat had taught lessons that training could never provide. As Bernard McElwaine observed after their stint at le Mesnil-Patry, "Our ears are getting tuned to off-stage noises. It saves a lot of ducking when you can tell a Jerry from one of ours." And the men of the NSR, like all other soldiers, had learned how to turn a slit trench into a comfortable home and still keep it largely concealed from the enemy.

At 1400 hours on June 27, the North Shore left le Mesnil-Patry and the war for a few days and marched north to a rest area at Bouanville in the Mue River valley. The relief was palpable. As the sound of the guns grew faint, Padre Hickey noticed that his teeth chattered when he talked. He mentioned it to Doc Patterson, who replied simply, "So are mine; everyone's teeth are chattering."

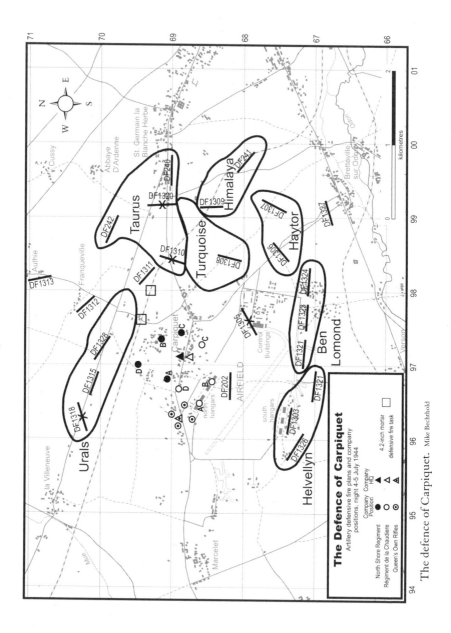

The defence of Carpiquet. Mike Bechthold

The Defence of Carpiquet
Artillery defensive fire plans and company
positions, night 4–5 July 1944

Chapter Five

Carpiquet

By late June 1944, the Normandy campaign was stalled. In the Anglo-Canadian sector the Germans held the line with a cordon of Panzer divisions, including eighty percent of their tanks. The Americans west of Bayeux, despite capturing the thinly garrisoned Cotentin Peninsula, were stymied by tenacious defenders hidden within an intricate network of hedgerows and bog. The Allied beachhead remained small, and the great storm of June 19-23 seriously delayed the buildup. For the British, in particular, hopes of breaking the stalemate and establishing a war of movement died on June 30. On that day, Operation EPSOM ground to a halt following fierce counter-attacks by the newly arrived 2nd SS Panzer Corps. It was now clear that there was no "easy" way around Caen. The collapse of EPSOM in the valley of the Odon and the realization that Caen would have to be taken by direct assault led to the decision to capture Carpiquet. And it was at Carpiquet that the "old" North Shore Regiment died.

None of this had quite been decided when the NSR and the rest of the 8th Brigade arrived at Bouanville late on the twenty-seventh for a break. Padre Hickey later described these days as ones of rest, but his memory was faulty. The very next day, while the men relaxed, senior officers were briefed on Operation

Ottawa, a proposed attack by 8th Brigade on the airfield and village of Carpiquet in direct support of the faltering British attack across the Odon River. With British troops now down in the river valley west of Verson and heavily engaged in the burning wheat fields on the northern slopes of Hill 112, Germans on the southern lip of the plateau that held the Carpiquet airfield could overlook them from the side and rear. Operation Ottawa was intended to clear that spur of land where Carpiquet sits in order to ease pressure on the British VIIIth Corps. And so on the twenty-ninth, the NSR marched back to Bretteville-l'Orgueilleuse to launch Operation Ottawa, only to redeploy immediately just to the east at la Villeneuve in response to a threatened German breakthrough. When the German attack failed and the British abandoned attempts to drive south of the Odon River, Operation Ottawa was abandoned. The NSR and the other battalions of the 8th Brigade marched back to Bouanville for a few more days of rest.

Within days the plan to capture the village and airport of Carpiquet was resuscitated, in the words of the Canadian official history in a "more robust form," as Operation Windsor. Persistent demands from VIIIth Corps to deny the Germans direct observation of their positions in the Odon River valley was one reason. However, if Carpiquet, its airport, and the control buildings to the southeast on the fifty-metre contour line could be taken, the Allies would have direct observation into Caen and the rear areas of the German positions guarding it to the north. For all these reasons, senior Anglo-Canadian officers also understood that any attack at Carpiquet would draw the Germans into fierce counter-attacks; that was their well-known doctrine. And so, an attack on Carpiquet served three purposes: it would eliminate German oversight of VIIIth Corps positions, give the Allies critical direct observation over German positions in and around Caen, and permit the destruction of German reserves in the Caen area prior to the main attack on the city. In many ways, the attack on Carpiquet was akin to poking a stick into a wasp's nest; everyone knew what would happen next. The job fell to 8th Brigade and its supporting troops, along with one battalion (the Royal Winnipeg Rifles) from 7th Brigade. Thus, while the 811 officers and men of the North Shore caught up on their administrative chores, cleaned their weapons, and skylarked around Bouanville, preparations for Operation WINDSOR began in earnest.

The target of Operation WINDSOR was actually threefold: the sprawling village of Carpiquet and the adjacent northern hangers of the airfield; the airport control buildings at the eastern end of the airfield; and the hangers and bunker complex on the southside. The job of taking the southside hangers and bunkers, from which the Germans could observe VIIIth Corps in the Odon Valley, was assigned to the RWR, supported by tanks, tank destroyers, and AVREs. The main attack on the village, the northern hangers, and the control buildings belonged to the 8th Brigade and was to be done in two phases. In phase one, the NSR and Chaudières would capture the village and northern hangers with help from two squadrons of Fort Garry tanks, two troops of AVREs, one squadron of Crocodile flame-throwing tanks, and two troops of M-10 tank destroyers. Once the NSR and Chauds had secured the village, phase two would see the QOR and a squadron of tanks capture the control buildings southeast of the village and occupy positions along the fifty-metre contour line overlooking Caen.

Since the objectives of Operation WINDSOR lay 2,500 metres forward of Canadian lines across open and largely flat ground, there was no quick and easy way to get there. Tactical surprise was impossible. To help the battalions get forward, take their objectives, and then hold them, the 4th Army Group, Royal Artillery (4 AGRA) — the artillery organization of 2nd British Army, of which the Canadians were a part — laid on a massive fire plan of over five hundred guns, essentially every gun in Normandy that could reach the battlefield. This included over fifteen field regiments, a dozen medium and at least one heavy regiment, and the 16-inch guns of the battleship HMS *Rodney* and the 15-inch guns of the monitor HMS *Roberts*. A program of air attacks was also laid on, and two squadrons of rocket-firing Typhoon aircraft were assigned to support the attack. The heaviest guns fired on strongpoints such as the village and bunkers, or fired counter-battery programs to silence the German artillery, while

Carpiquet, July 6, 1944. The North Shore start line lay in the top left hand corner of the photo. The airport complex south of the main road was the Chaudières objective, while a small portion of the control buildings — the Queen's Own objective — can be seen in the bottom right hand corner of the photo. The open but clearly defined nature of the northern portion of the village, captured and held by the North Shore, is shown clearly here. LCMSDS

the lighter field artillery regiments provided barrages that — much like in the Great War — "walked" the infantry forward across the open fields and then supported them closely as they fought through the village.

While all this was going on, the medium machine guns and big 4.2-inch mortars of the 8th Brigade's own support battalion, the Cameron Highlanders of Ottawa, were to fire on selected points on the left flank of the 8th Brigade attack and the hangers in front of the RWR. Meanwhile, north of the Carpiquet battlefield, feints and raids were to be conducted by the 7th and 9th Canadian Infantry Brigades to draw enemy fire and reserves into the area around Authie and Buron. All things considered, it looked like a good plan. It was certainly powerful, and there was no question it would get the Germans' attention.

The 12th SS Panzer Division, Hitler Youth, of the 1st SS Panzer Corps, with supporting elements from other formations, held the Carpiquet front. Composed of a lethal mixture of battle-hardened officers and non-commissioned officers from the 1st SS Panzer Division, Liebstandarte Adolph Hitler, and selected seventeen-year olds from the Hitler Youth movement, the 12th SS had a reputation for fanatical fighting. Three battalions of its 25th Panzergrenadier (PzG) Regiment (the equivalent of an Anglo-Canadian brigade) held positions in front of the 7th and 9th Canadian Brigades from Franqueville to St. Contest. The 25th PzG, on high ground north of the railway line and Route National 13, overlooked the whole Carpiquet battlefield, especially the route followed and positions occupied by the NSR. The actual objectives of Operation WINDSOR were held by what was left of the 3rd Battalion of the 26th PzG Regiment, (3/26th), a regiment depleted by recent fighting. One company and an additional platoon (about 150 men) were in Carpiquet village, and two companies less a platoon held the southern hangers.

Historians typically point to the disparity between the Canadian force attacking Carpiquet and its defenders as evidence of overwhelming Allied superiority in numbers and weapons, and the tactical incompetence of the Anglo-Canadians. But like the

Canadian 8th Brigade, the 3/26th PzG Regiment did not fight alone. In addition to fire from flanking formations, it was powerfully supported by tanks and artillery. In immediate support from its own division, the 3/26th had four 88-mm guns sited near St. Germaine-la-Blanche-Herbe to cover the eastern end of the village, five Mk IV tanks, and a company (about twelve by this stage) of Panther tanks, a battalion of artillery (typically twelve guns), elements of the 83rd Werfer Regiment (50-kg rocket projectors), plus its own battalion mortars. Moreover, as the attackers would discover, virtually every gun in 1st SS Panzer Corps was within range of the battlefield, and the Germans had no evident shortage of ammunition.

It is clear from the dispositions of the 12th SS that the Germans had no intention of trying to hold Carpiquet village in force against an attack that they knew was coming. The pattern of Allied counter-battery fire, reconnaissance patrols, and air strikes, as well as other information, indicated as early as July 2 that Carpiquet was next. The massive concrete bunkers at the southern hangers, supported by direct tank fire from across the airfield and artillery in the dead ground to the south, garrisoned by two companies and with a company of Panther tanks ready to counterattack, could probably be held. The village would bear the brunt of the Canadian attack, and it could be temporarily given up. The Canadian assault would have to come across two and a half kilometres of open ground that was under observation and could be swept by massive firepower. Should the Canadians succeed in taking the village, they would be left in possession of a narrow salient overlooked from three sides by the Germans. As their doctrine prescribed, the Germans would then pound the Canadian forward positions with a crushing weight of fire and counter-attack to recapture the village from the dazed defenders.

While Anglo-Canadian gunners calculated the details of the fire plan, sweating service corps personnel dumped ammunition around gun positions, and officers poured over patrol reports and aerial photographs, the NSR "rested" at Bouanville. Its task as a reserve battalion meant that it still had much to do, including route planning for counter-attacks and preparing defended positions. It also remained well within range of enemy guns, some directed at it specifically, which caused a few casualties, and others simply harassing the Allied beachhead. As a result, on July 2, it suffered casualties even in this rest area when enemy shells air burst over A Company's positions. On that same day, the battalion ordered special stores for the upcoming battle. These included 450 rolls of concertina wire, 450 pickets, 75 rolls of barbed wire, and 1,500 anti-personnel mines: all defensive material, which says a very great deal about what the NSR thought was going to happen once they got into Carpiquet.

Events began to unfold the next day. At 1130 hours on July 3, Lieutenant-Colonel Buell attended a brigade Orders Group, and at 1500 the NSR began its move forward to la Villeneuve. Battalion headquarters set up in the walled grounds of the château (which still stands) just north of the rail line. Company commanders assembled there for the final briefing at 1830 hours.

In 1944, Carpiquet was a sprawling village surrounded by open farm-land and a major airport. A small business core ran along the main road adjacent to the airport, while to the north a loose cluster of farm build-ings, homes, and garden plots centred around the church. The northern section of the village was well defined by a perimeter of roads and tree lines, giving good cover and fields of fire for defenders. This portion of Carpiquet was assigned to the North Shore. Buell's plan called for an at-tack on a two-company front roughly half a kilometre in length, with D on the left and A on the right leading and B and C companies following. Their start line lay in the field south of the Caen-Bayeux rail line, just to the east of the road running from la Villeneuve to Marcelet. D Company had the rail line to its left for the whole distance to the walls of the village, while the axis of advance for the battalion was defined by two farm-track junctions in the midst of a huge field of standing wheat. The lead companies were to clear the first half of the northern part of Carpiquet, then let the reserve companies pass through to tackle the rest of the village. On the NSR's right, the Chaudières, also with two companies up and two following, conformed to the NSR align-ment from its start line at Marcelet. Its axis of

Major J.E. Anderson, commander of A Company at Carpiquet. 2RNBR

advance was better defined, being the main road between Marcelet and Carpiquet itself. Further south, on the other side of Marcelet, the RWR lined up for its attack on the southern hangers.

The NSR got little rest the night before the assault. All reflected on the perils of attacking and many had premonitions of death. Of the three other men in Lieutenant Chester MacRae's slit trench in the château grounds, two felt that July 4 would be their last day. In the end, all but MacRae died. The six Acadians from northeastern New Brunswick in Omer Larocque's group fared a little better: only three died, but everyone else was wounded. The sudden arrival of mail that night added a tinge of sadness to the whole affair. Lieutenant Paul McCann and his brother Joe, several years older and a corporal, had just celebrated birthdays in late June, and as they huddled in a slit tench in the château grounds, they received a parcel from home. All the edibles immediately went into pockets for later — they would be needed. But it's not clear what the McCann boys did with the two pairs of flannel pyjamas. "We had a good laugh," Paul McCann wrote after the war, "but the pangs of nostalgia that moment engendered will be with me to my dying day."

Reveille came early, at 0230 hours on July 4, with breakfast at 0300. The night was very dark and most men ate in silence. Major Ernie Anderson, Captain Fred Moar, his new second in command, CSM Fenton Daley, and the three platoon commanders of A Company used the hood of a jeep as a table and dined on canned sausages. The only thing Anderson could recall anyone saying was Daley's speculation on when they would get a chance to eat again. In later years, Anderson remembered it as a quiet night. Clint Gammon's recollection was starkly different. "We were shelled quite heavily," Gammon recalled. "Heine making every effort to break us while in the assembly area." We do know that German mortar fire on the likely Canadian assembly areas began about 0400, when the supporting tanks began to move. Clearly the attack would not be a surprise.

As the first German mortar bombs began to land, A Company filed out of the château grounds onto the highway at la Villeneuve and moved south towards the railway underpass. Other companies followed at five-minute intervals. "On the way we passed a Field Ambulance setting up for service," Anderson recalled. The medics would have much to do that day. At the railway underpass they were met by an intelligence corps sergeant who was to guide them to the start line, which had been taped during the night. Anderson told him not to bother, they knew where to go: only two to four hundred yards south of the rail line. D Company had less distance to go, just through the underpass and a sharp turn left. But it was not until 0450 — with only ten minutes to spare — that the company was deployed and ready. Like A Company, D had two platoons up, headquarters, and one behind, and a small screen just in front to guard against surprises.

On the morning of July 4, the NSR had everyone in line waiting to go. The practice of a "left out of battle" (LOB) party — some key personnel and a certain percentage of each company left behind to provide a cadre for rebuilding should things go badly — was not yet commonplace. Returns for July 1 show the battalion had been at nearly full strength: thirty-seven officers and 801 non-commissioned officers and men, just ten privates and a couple of sergeants below their War Establishment.

The famous CBC radio reporter Matthew Halton, recording a broadcast of the start of the Carpiquet battle, commented on the sudden transformation of the scene from one of quiet anticipation to a deafening roar as five hundred guns opened fire at 0500 hours. Men in the assault companies had a similar impression. As Major Anderson recalled, the artillery fire "was awe inspiring, to say the least — one minute we were in a

quiet and peaceful countryside with dawn just breaking; the next, the ground under us shaking from the bursts of shells — field, medium, and heavy." According to Major Gammon of D Company, "At zero hour the whole horizon in a semi-circle behind us became a blaze when the artillery opened up." Anderson saw the 16-inch shells of the battleship *Rodney* bursting in the village and around the control buildings. So did Gunner Bill Milner, a New Brunswicker serving with the headquarters of 13th RCA. Milner witnessed the enormous shells of *Rodney* sending whole trees, vehicles "and all these little figures in grey greatcoats" flying through the air. As the medium and heavy regiments played on the village and strongpoints, the supporting fire for the infantry — a linear barrage stretching from the railway to well south of the Marcelet-Carpiquet road — began to land two hundred yards in front of the start line. The barrage was to stay in place for ten minutes and then start moving across the field in one hundred yard "lifts" every three minutes: it was the infantry's task to stay as close as possible to the barrage as it moved forward.

Problems arose immediately. While A Company had waited some distance back from the start line and used the ten-minute initial barrage as a signal to close up to its start line, D Company deployed forward and may have gotten caught in its own supporting fire. Gammon recalled that the first rounds of the supporting barrage landed as expected, two hundred yards ahead of them. But soon shells began to fall on his reserve platoon, and eventually the whole company was engulfed in explosions. The NSR War Diary speculated that Allied artillery fell short during the opening barrage, and some in the regiment believed that the start and barrage lines had been improperly taped. But it was just as likely that D Company was struck by German fire, which we now know was quickly targeted on the assault companies that were known to be two hundred yards behind the Allied barrage. Such predictability — and susceptibility to exploitation — was one of the major problems of fixed, linear barrages and why Carpiquet was one of the last times they were used. Any gunner could have recognized what was happening, and it was a simple matter to lay down a counter-barrage just behind the Canadian barrage and punish the attacker all the way to his objective. This is likely what happened to the NSR on the morning of July 4, 1944.

As a result, D Company — overlooked by the enemy from high ground north of the rail line — suffered heavily even before it started to move. Gammon set off to check on his reserve platoon when shells began to land among his company, then immediately returned to the lead platoons. By the time he got back "the enemy counter-barrage was really coming down and a lot of my men were dead or wounded. . . . It looked for a while as if we would never get off the start line." Gammon solved the problem by hugging his own barrage tighter, thereby keeping just ahead of the German fire. However, many men never took a step forward. Much of the German fire fell heaviest on the reserve companies. "Within minutes of the opening salvoes the Moaning Minnies [*Nebelwerfer* rockets] and crying for help began and we had no choice but to take it," Lieutenant C.F. Richardson of B Company explained. Only twenty of his thirty-five men crossed the start line. Sergeant Gavin Hickey of the mortar platoon travelling with B Company said later, "It gave us an awful, helpless feeling to see enemy artillery fire smashing through the ranks, wounding and killing, disorganizing the companies." Padre Hickey found the remnants of B Company after the barrage had moved on. "They had taken the brunt of the shelling," he wrote. "Everywhere men lay dead or dying. I anointed about thirty right there."

The NSR began crossing the fields towards Carpiquet at 0512, but the situation improved only slightly. The shelling raised a tremendous dust cloud, and, in Sergeant Fenton Daley's words, "The wheat was chewed off at ground level by artillery fire and still steaming." Only men led by those with compasses could keep their bearing. According to Major Anderson, "The advance through the grain fields to Carpiquet was little short of hell." On one occasion, Anderson saw one of his forward platoons crossing behind him at right angles to the axis of advance and then simply disappear into the smoke. Without their officer, who was mortally wounded, they had no idea where they were going. Lieutenant Richardson of

B Company started off with Paul McCann's platoon on his right, and when Richardson next met McCann about halfway across, the latter was on Richardson's left. Through the smoke and din of battle men kept going. When Sergeant Daley cleared the smoke just short of the village, he saw a lone figure to his right who called out, "I'm the only one left in our platoon!" before plunging into the village to continue the fight.

Men went down on all sides, mostly from artillery and other forms of indirect fire, but some were shot by Germans in the outpost line. By Ernie Anderson's estimation, there were about seventy Hitler Youth in the field in front of Carpiquet, holding machine-gun positions and trenches. All the way across that two and a half kilometre stretch, the NSR "flushed out or killed enemy who had stayed in the slit trenches until the last moment." One German soldier who lived to tell his story later recalled being almost completely buried by a Canadian tank. The tank's crew saw Karl-Heinz Wambach fire a green flare — a signal for artillery support — when they were too close to fire at him. So the tank charged Wambach's trench, turned a full circle around it, and filled the trench with soil spilling from its tracks before going on. Buried to his chest, Wambach had dug himself free to his hips when he suddenly heard, "SS Bastard, hands up!" The NSR soldiers unceremoniously pulled Wambach free, tied his hands, punched him in the face, herded him back to the rear, prodding none too gently with rifle butts, and left him tied to a tree amid mortar fire. Wambach later complained of his treatment, but given the way Canadians felt about the 12th SS, he got off lucky. He was fortunate, too, not to get buried alive in the sandy soil of Carpiquet, a common fate on both sides of the battle.

The outposts of the 3rd Company of the 3/26th PzG Regiment in the open fields in front of Carpiquet were smothered by the withering fire. Without it, Anderson claimed, the attacking battalions would never have made it to the village through the outpost line. Those Germans left to resist, like Wambach, were dealt with by the NSR, or by the Fort Garry tanks who followed the infantry so closely that their fire passed just overhead of the leading waves. In the end, thirty-five dazed POWs were recovered from the NSR portion of the field, and a further thirty-five enemy dead left behind.

Among the many acts of bravery and leadership displayed during the advance, the NSR regimental history singled out Corporal Eddie Hosford as "one of the real heroes." Almost from the outset, casualties in his platoon left him in charge. Hosford rose to the occasion, leading his men towards Carpiquet, stopping to help the wounded, including one man whose arm was severed by a shell splinter: Corporal Hosford tied a strip of minetape on the stump as a tourniquet and sent the man back. When a machine gun stopped his company on the outskirts of the village, Hosford selected three other men and led the attack that captured the position. "This," Will Bird observed, "allowed the company to proceed to its objective," where Hosford organized the deployment of what remained of his platoon.

By the time the NSR reached the western edge of Carpiquet, the 2,500 metres back to its start line was a smouldering ruin littered with shell holes, wrecked vehicles, bodies, and a trail of rifles stuck into the ground with Canadian helmets on the top. These not only helped the stretcher bearers recover the wounded, they also prevented tanks from running over them. Captain W. B. Nixon of the 12th Field Regiment, RCA, whose guns supported the NSR that day, estimated that "infantry casualties amounted to approximately forty percent" just getting into the village. Major Anderson spoke for the whole battalion when he later wrote:

> I am sure that at some time during the attack every man felt he could not go on. Men were being killed or wounded on all sides and the advance seemed pointless as well as hopeless. I never realized until the attack at Carpiquet how far discipline, pride of unit and, above all, pride in oneself and family can carry a man even when each step forward meant possible death.

When A Company finally reached the airport hangers at the western edge of the village, "a cheer went up" as the men swept the last few yards to the comparative shelter of the stone wall. It was now 0625 — well over an hour after the attack started — and the leading companies finally reported themselves at Carpiquet. There they had to wait for a full twenty minutes as the artillery pounded the western edge of the village. In retrospect this, too, was a mistake. Not only did it waste time when it was likely that the assault battalions could have stormed through, but, at least among the NSR, the shells exploding in the tall trees rained shrapnel down on it and caused more casualties. Finally, at about 0710, the barrage moved again, and the Canadians surged into the village. Now a new form of hell began.

No coherent account of the actual capture of Carpiquet village has ever been written, nor does the surviving documentation lend itself to constructing one. The village was already smashed by artillery gunfire. While the NSR and Chaudières paused at the western edge to let their supporting fire play across the rubble, the surviving German defenders struggled to dig themselves and their weapons out of collapsed buildings and trenches. German accounts describe a "bitter battle for the town" in which the British Crocodile flame-throwing tanks supporting the Chaudières were decisive in the battle for the northern hangers. But North Shore accounts do not support the view that there was much of a battle for the northern section of the village, perhaps because there were so few Hitler Youth left. According to citizens who remained in Carpiquet, most of its garrison ran away. CSM Rod Johnson recalled that his men "charged into Carpiquet eagerly but the Jerry there had beat it." Captain J.A. Currie, commanding the carrier platoon, agreed that it was over quickly: "It was house-to-house clearance and soon over." As Sergeant Gavin Hickey of B Company concluded, "It was a terrible trip through the grain but when we reached Carpiquet the Germans had moved out and there were only some French in the underground shelters." In any event, the NSR reported its section of Carpiquet captured at 0812 hours. Twenty Germans were captured in the process; the number of dead found is unrecorded.

While the NSR and Chauds consolidated in Carpiquet, the first attempt by the Royal Winnipeg Rifles to capture the southern hangers on the far side of the airfield failed in the face of stiff resistance. The Winnipegs made it across their own two kilometres of open ground to the southern hangers and bunker complex by 0900. But no amount of artillery, short of a direct hit by one of the *Rodney*'s 16-inch shells, could penetrate the bunkers where the Germans sheltered (although they complained of large chunks of concrete falling off the inside from shell blasts). For four hours, the RWR tried to winkle the Germans out, while tanks firing from the far side of the airfield destroyed the Winnipegs' supporting tanks and AVREs and the artillery of the 12th SS smothered the position with defensive fire. Unable to do anything at all, the RWR retreated at 1300 to lick its wounds and prepare for another try.

By 1100 hours, the village of Carpiquet was secure enough for 8th Brigade to commence phase two: the capture of the control buildings in the southeast corner of the airfield by the Queen's Own Rifles. As it turned out, it had to fight its way into Carpiquet along the main road through positions overrun but not fully cleared by the Chaudières. Finally, supported by Fort Garry tanks, the QOR set out from the eastern edge of Carpiquet for the control buildings across five hundred metres of open ground. The 88-mm guns at St. Germain quickly destroyed the tanks, and the open ground between the village and control buildings was so swept by fire that the attack was abandoned just as quickly as it started. With that, phase two was abandoned, and the QOR moved to a reserve position at the western entrance to the village. The 8th Brigade contented itself with holding Carpiquet village, while the RWR organized a second attack on the southern hangers.

For the rest of July 4, 1944, what was left of the NSR consolidated its positions in the northern section of the village: D Company, down to half strength, held the northern apex near the railway line; B Company, slightly better off, held the sector east of the church; C Company, with only fifty all ranks, was between B and A Company of the Chaudières holding the southeastern portion of the village across the main road; A Company was in reserve near the centre of the village. Buell called for anti-tank guns at 0835, but the battalion's guns were already on the move. It is unclear where these were deployed, but the four M-10 tank destroyers from the 3rd Anti-

Six-pounder gun of the 3rd Anti-Tank Regiment, RCA, moves through Carpiquet, July 1944. LAC PA-132873

Tank Regiment, RCA, were dug in well forward: two with B Company and two with C Company. The medium machine guns of the Camerons were deployed in D Company's area to sweep along the rail line and in front of D and B companies. Battalion mortars were deployed near a hanger on the western edge of the village. "The consolidation and the preparations made were a credit to the tactical skill of our beloved Lieutenant-Colonel Buell," Paul McCann recalled. Under constant shellfire and the threat of enemy attack, Buell was everywhere, visiting the company positions once or twice during the day.

Much of the shelling on the fourth came from *Nebelwerfers* — known to the Allies as Moaning Minnies because of the sound of their rocket motors — of the 1st SS Corps heavy artillery. These were located near the southern hangers and defied attempts by Allied artillery and air-power to silence them. The 50-kg charges of Moaning Minnies pounded Carpiquet relentlessly and the NSR soon found itself digging its own men out of collapsed buildings. Rod Johnson was sitting in his company HQ that afternoon when a *Nebelwerfer* rocket struck the building. The cut stone and brick simply fell in around them, trapping Johnson and several men — one of them for the second time that day. They were able to hear voices outside, as others dug to free them. However, when the rubble began to collapse around the rescuers, Johnson heard one say, "All in there are gone. It's no use to dig." It took Johnson and the others more than an hour to get out. "It was the worst hour I had in France," Johnson later remembered, "It was like digging out of a grave." Sergeant Fulton Noye of C Company had three buildings destroyed around him in the first two days. When signalman Percy Scott's bunker took a direct hit and buried everyone in it, he was saved by a blanket that fell over his face. By the time his friend Harold Arseneau reached Scott he looked more dead than alive. As Arseneau gently brushed the dirt from his face, Scott opened his eyes and said coolly, "Well, what are you looking at? Dig me out!"

Finding and silencing the German fire proved to be almost impossible. Gunner Bill Milner of 13th RCA recalled sheltering in a Carpiquet basement when a small figure burst through the door, tumbled down the steps, and landed in a heap on the floor amid a cloud of red dust from blasted roof tiles. It was Lieutenant-Colonel Freddie le P.T. Clifford, Milner's commanding officer, clutching a field service notepad in his hand. Clifford had been out trying to estimate German mortar positions, and he immediately stepped toward the radio to pass along the map references. There is

Major R.H. Daughney, on the left, inspects a German submachine gun brought back by Captain R.E. Bolt, on the right, from a patrol. Bolt joined the NSR on July 5 in Carpiquet. IWM

no evidence that Clifford's efforts were successful, but Milner was deeply impressed with his courage and professionalism.

Captain Phillip Oland, another New Brunswicker and a FOO with 12th RCA, had no better luck trying to stop the tank fire that whittled away at the NSR position on July 4. He arrived in the afternoon having brought his Sherman tank across the open road from Marcelet at 30 mph. Oland immediately joined Major Daughney's C Company on the eastern edge of the village. Since Oland and Daughney were old classmates from the University of New Brunswick, a simple "Hello Ralph!" sufficed as an introduction. A thousand yards in front of Daughney's position, three or four tanks were, in Oland's words, "firing away at our hedgerows with 88s." But every time Oland engaged them with his guns, the tanks slipped back behind the crest and popped up in a new spot; the best he could do was harass them. However, artillery kept a curtain of fire around Carpiquet during the day, and British rocket-firing Typhoons hunted and attacked German positions and vehicles.

The Germans did everything they could to weaken the defenders and destroy their resolve in advance of their major counter-attack. They understood clearly the implications of the Canadian presence in Carpiquet: it made the German line north of Caen untenable. Carpiquet had to be retaken or Caen was lost. The German task was made easier by the second and final failure of the Winnipegs to take the southern hangers, which started at 1600. Once again, the RWR reached their objective, but the western Canadians were unable to get at the Germans hiding in the concrete; and once again, they were driven off by German fire. Defence of those positions cost the Germans dearly: 150 killed, wounded, and missing, twenty more than the attacking RWR. However, with the southern hangers still in German hands, the 8th Brigade position in Carpiquet village now formed a narrow salient deep within enemy lines. It was in danger of falling to a concerted attack.

The task of retaking Carpiquet fell to the 1st PanzerGrenadier Regiment of the 1st SS Panzer Division, Leibstandarte Adolph Hitler (LAH). The LAH began as Hitler's personal guard and was now the elite of the Nazi party's armed forces. It had spent much of the war on the eastern front engaged in battles of astonishing brutality. As the personal guard of the Nazi leader, the LAH offered little mercy to its opponents and received little from the Russians in return. Much of their ethos was transferred to the 12th SS Hitler Youth, which was created in 1942 as a unique combination of LAH officers and senior NCOs and fanatical teenage Nazis. In late June 1944, the LAH returned to Normandy (where it had served briefly in late 1942), and on July 4, they and the 12th SS combined to form a new 1st SS Panzer Corps. By then, as Brigadier Michael Reynolds has written, the LAH "had developed their own philosophy of soldiering. It glorified fighting for fighting's sake. Its members had little regard for life, either their own or that of anyone else." Fresh from the eastern front, the SS were accustomed to bullying the Russians with a freewheeling, reckless style of combat, but they were to get a rude shock in their first battle with Canadians.

As the long Norman summer twilight dwindled, no one in the NSR or the Chaudières and their supporting units misunderstood what the next phase of the battle involved. The North Shore War Diary recorded at the end of July 4 that although they were "being constantly shelled and suffering many casualties there was no thought of withdrawal." In fact, as shadows deepened and darkness crept over the smoking ruins of Carpiquet, the NSR

The heart of old Carpiquet after the battle, looking southeast from the
steeple of St. Martin's Church. B Company's headquarters was in this part
of town. C Company occupied positions amid the hedges at the top of the
photo. Ville de Carpiquet

made its final preparations for the looming attack, laying barbed wire obstacles and improvised minefields in front of their company positions. At the same time, the LAH's 3rd Battalion, 1st PzG Regiment (3/1st) assembled on the other side of Route 13 around the hamlet of Franqueville, and the 1/1st moved into positions on the eastern edge of the airfield near the control buildings.

The twilight also allowed Padre Hickey and Major Lockwood to lead a burial party back onto the shattered plain west of Carpiquet. Hickey recollected that "in the gathering dusk," the field looked much like any at home, until you looked a little closer: "the wheat was trampled into the earth; the ground was torn by shell holes; and everywhere you could see the pale, upturned faces of the dead. That night alone we buried forty — Carpiquet was the graveyard of the regiment." In all, 170 men of the NSR had fallen on July 4, 1944, forty-six of them dead. It proved to be the worst day of the war for the regiment.

But Carpiquet was also the North Shore Regiment's greatest moment. With rifle companies down to about half strength, overlooked and blasted from three sides by everything the elite Nazi forces could throw at them, the NSR was about to win one of its most important victories. For about six hours in the early morning of July 5, 1944, Hitler's personal guard launched a series of attacks in a desperate effort to drive the Canadians out of the village. Four out of five of these fell on the North Shore, and the fifth one partly so. All of them failed, and the Germans were thrown back with heavy casualties. When it was over, the Canadians still held Carpiquet, and the Germans had spent their last remaining operational reserve in the Caen sector.

The anticipated counter-attack began at 0130 hours with a heavy barrage. What remained of the village was set alight, the flames encouraged by the 50-kg rockets filled with flammable oil fired by the *Nebelwerfer* regiment. Men of the SS were told that the Canadians would be unable to withstand the shelling and would be gone by the time they got to the village. They were wrong.

Shortly after 0200 the 3rd battalion, 1st

Vickers medium machine gun of the Cameron Highlanders of Ottawa, during the final pre-invasion exercise in April 1944. LAC

SS PzG Regiment, supported by ten tanks, began to move south across Route 13 on either side of the road from Franqueville. Almost immediately the leading company was struck by artillery fire and suffered heavy casualties. The Germans believed that this fire came from their own supporting artillery, but the spot was marked as "defensive fire" task 1312 by Canadian gunners and it was probably Anglo-Canadian shells that shattered the leading company. No. 3 Company now took the lead, and the SS pressed on. According to German accounts, they were stopped again at the railway by withering Canadian fire. "The 'Tommies' had woken-up, our element of surprise had gone to hell," Sturmann Gerhard Franz later recalled. "Violent defensive fire from the right and dead ahead hammered us. Our only reference points were the enemy muzzle flashes: we had to move forward precisely into that!" Much of the fire at the rail line probably came from the Camerons' machine guns, sited with D Company to the west, and from their 4.2-inch mortars, since the Camerons had the point marked for their own defensive fire task.

North Shore accounts all agree that the 3/1st SS was finally stopped at the edge of the village by a sudden and staggering burst of fire. According to Lieutenant McCann, the NSR watched the Germans advancing over the lip of the hill south of Franqueville, across the road and rail line, and into the low ground just north of Carpiquet. Artillery fire played on them, and Philip Oland called down three "SOS" barrages on the Germans at different stages when it appeared they were going to overrun the NSR. But the North Shore and tanks of the Fort Garry Horse held their fire. Those waiting included an M-10 tank destroyer of the 105th Battery RCA that had been slipped unseen into an ambush position at the railway crossing in the NSR's D Company sector.

By staying quiet, McCann said after the war, the Canadians "sucked wave after wave of Jerry infantry into the hollow where the withering cross fire of the Camerons cut off any hope of escape." Once committed to the attack, the SS never faltered. "By the time our signal was given they were right on our doorsteps," McCann recalled, "so out went the grenades followed by a withering small-arms fire that saw the barrels of Bren guns get white hot before the show was over. There were no casualties among my men but Jerry took a murderous beating and very few of their attacking force got back to their line." According to Major Bill Harvey, the Germans were so close when the NSR opened fire that it "almost lifted the advancing men from the ground. They were cut to pieces, and some had got so near, men in our trenches could almost reach out and touch the bodies." With this, the attackers broke and ran, leaving at least a hundred dead and wounded in front of B Company. Canadian casualties were negligible. The M-10 waiting by the railway crossing claimed three of the ten Panther tanks.

The second major attack appeared at 0530 hours, when, according to the War Diary, B Company "reported 25 to 30 Enemy tanks attacking from East of their position." Pleas to have this force struck by medium artillery on an urgent basis were made, and the attack was broken up by artillery fire that destroyed two of the tanks. By 0540 the Germans had retreated to hull-down positions near the quarries due east of B Company, where the rail line and the road to Caen intersected. The Germans tried two more times to attack from that area, at 0610 and 0650: both times they were forced back by small arms, artillery, and tank fire. By 0715, the NSR reported the situation in B Company sector "under control," and commented on the "very satisfactory" artillery support.

The only counter-attack on Carpiquet by the SS to achieve anything noteworthy began at 0725 on July 5. A force of at least six Panther tanks and supporting infantry overran a forward platoon of A Company of the Chaudières and their anti-tank guns at the eastern edge of the village, just to the right of C Company of the NSR. This started something of a rout on the flank of the weakest part of the NSR line. When Lieutenant Chester MacRae was asked the previous night to check on the state of the company he found only forty-one men and two officers — Major Daughney and himself — still standing. There was no company head-quarters, except for Daughney, and one platoon had only two men left. The collapse of the forward elements of Chaudières to its right put C Company in a perilous state.

While MacRae reoriented C Company's defences to deal with the new threat, Daughney summoned several M-10 tank destroyers, arranged for supporting artillery fire, and then, as Phillip Oland recalled, "grabbed a PIAT gun and said that he would try to get one of the tanks." Until help arrived things were hot along C Company's new southern flank, which was swept by fire from the Panthers. MacRae moved fearlessly among his small groups of men, dodging machine-gun bullets and shellfire until one tank round exploded close enough to knock him out for a few minutes. When he regained consciousness, MacRae went back to work and refused to be relieved until the enemy was driven out. According to Oland, it was the "constant firing by the personnel of this company" that prevented it from being overrun. When the M-10s finally arrived, three Panthers were destroyed in quick order, while the NSR's own reserves from A Company stabilized the situation. Pounded mercilessly by Canadian artillery fire directed by Oland, hunted by tank killers, and pressed by all three 8th Brigade battalions, the Germans withdrew to the comparative safety of the quarries again. Major Daughney reorganized the anti-tank platoon of the Chaudières before returning to the NSR lines. Lieutenant MacRae was evacuated and was later awarded a well-earned Military Cross for his efforts. C Company was now down to thirty-two men and its commanding officer.

At 0810 on the morning of July 5, the Queen's Own reported the situation in Carpiquet restored. The German attempt to retake Carpiquet was over, and the remnants of the 1st SS Division's force sheltering around the quarries — an area soon littered with fifteen wrecked tanks — was under attack from the air. Their only option now was withdrawal.

Operation WINDSOR is usually regarded as a dismal failure because the southern hangers and control buildings were not taken, and because Canadian casualties were so high compared to those of the Germans. And the Canadian assault on Carpiquet village itself is often viewed as an example of bungling Allied methods: four full battalions supported by massive firepower and tanks attacking a depleted German battalion resulting in minimal success and heavy losses. It is generally assumed that the Germans lost 155 men in the first two days of fighting at Carpiquet, a figure which contrasts sharply with the 377 Canadians who were killed, wounded, or missing.

However, although disappointing, particularly in its failure to secure the southern hangers, Operation WINDSOR was a significant tactical, operational, and even strategic success. Indeed, the battalions of the 8th Brigade held onto Carpiquet and drew both a maelstrom of fire and savage German counter-attack onto their position. At a certain level, that was entirely the point. The Allies, including those diehards of the NSR who made it to the village, knew that the Germans would fight fanatically to retake it. The SS at-

tackers in the early hours of July 5 were told that no one could withstand the constant shelling and that they would find Carpiquet empty. As Major J.A.L. Robichaud said, the Germans "got a very sad surprise."

Not only did the Germans fail to dislodge the Canadians from their salient, they also suffered heavily at Carpiquet. The figure of 155, routinely quoted by historians on both sides as the German count of killed, wounded, and missing, refers to only those admitted to by the 26th PzG Regiment of 12th SS, and is inaccurate. By some accounts, German losses around the southern hangers attacked by the RWR amounted to 150 men, while the reinforced third company of the 3/26th in the village was virtually annihilated: the NSR captured fifty-five and counted about thirty-five SS dead in the wheat field. How many died in the village is unknown, but there must have been some. Those figures amount to 240 from the 12th SS alone. More importantly, for some unknown reason, losses to the 1st SS Division during the morning of July 5 are never tallied in the Carpiquet figures. According to their own history, the 3rd Battalion of the 1st SS PzG Regiment lost 115 infantry (killed, wounded, and missing) plus about twenty tanks. This figure is corroborated by B Company of the NSR, who counted about one hundred dead and wounded in front of its position at dawn. These losses bring German casualties for July 4-5 to about 340. But the real figure is probably higher still. The Germans provide no casualty figures for their supporting tanks and other units, none from the three attacks by the 1st Battalion of the 1st SS PzG Regiment at all, and we can only speculate on the casualties from the artillery fire brought down on formations preparing to attack, such as the 3rd Company of the 3/1st SS just outside Franqueville at the start of the first attack. Based on all this, casualties on both sides were about even, and the SS paid dearly for their fanatical disregard for life, especially their own, and for their arrogance in the face of Anglo-Canadian defensive firepower.

More importantly, in trying to retake Carpiquet the Germans committed their only available operational reserve in the Caen sector, and it was destroyed. As the Canadian Army's official post-war narrative reveals, four out of five of these attacks fell on the North Shore Regiment, and the fifth was stopped by their intervention. It was their fire, and that of their supporting elements, that crushed the elite of Hitler's personal guard and shattered German hopes of holding Caen. The old North Shore may have died at Carpiquet, but it took a lot of Germans and its enemy's plans for the defence of Caen with them. As Major Bill Harvey reflected, "There was never the like of those North Shore men for sheer guts and durability."

The Place du Royal North Shore Regiment, Tailleville. Matt Symes

Conclusion

Bretteville-sur-Odon

The North Shore War Diary on the morning of July 5 records that the men were "sleepy and hungry" and although the "shelling from enemy mortars was heavy there was no let-down in Spirit." That shelling went on all through the day, diminishing somewhat after noon. By then, the Germans had decided that, since they could not retake Carpiquet, they would keep it under harassing fire while they reorganized their defences and prepared to abandon positions north and west of Caen. And so for the next four days, the NSR and the rest of the 8th Brigade hung on in Carpiquet and endured the constant, if somewhat lighter, shelling. The men lived a troglodyte existence, moving from trench to trench, keeping out of sight, constantly digging their friends out of collapsed buildings and defences, and enduring the steady drain on strength caused by the constant shell fire. Sergeant Rod Foran captured some of the spirit of the North Shore in the aftermath of the battle in his poem, "The Day A Robin Sang at Carpiquet," reproduced in the appendix.

Around suppertime on July 5, five officers and 120 men arrived in the shell-torn village as much needed reinforcements for the NSR. "So many reinforcements had come in that I did not know half my men," Lieutenant Paul McCann recalled. "Often there would be a dozen arrive at a company in the even-

North Shore graves, Beny-sur-Mer Commonwealth War Cemetery:
Private A.G. Maclean, July 6, 1944; Private E.L. Thomas, July 4, 1944;
Private J.W. Poirier, July 4, 1944; Private W.T. Lockhart, July 4, 1944;
Private B. LeBlanc, July 5, 1944. Matt Symes

ing and before morning half that dozen would be casualties." For all the
new men, Carpiquet was a brutal indoctrination. Padre Hickey later la-
mented that many of the men he met for the first time in the evening he
buried the next morning.

Relief only came with the main Anglo-Canadian assault on Caen,
which began on the evening of July 7, with a thousand Lancaster bombers pounding the northern outskirts of the city. This was, according to
the War Diary, a "great morale builder" for the troops. The next day,
forward observers from the artillery operating in Carpiquet were able to
engage good targets as German forces on the plain to the north moved in

response to the Canadian attack sweeping down from Buron and Cairon. This ability to look into the rear of the German defences was what made Carpiquet so vital. Although Caen north of the Orne river fell on the eighth, Carpiquet was still under fire on July 9 when Lieutenant-Colonel Buell was ordered to moved his battalion forward to occupy the village of Bretteville-sur-Odon in the valley to the southeast. The advance began in mid-afternoon, and with that the NSR left Carpiquet for good.

The memory of those seven days, and the legacy of 289 men lost — seventy-seven of them dead — would remain forever. In regimental lore, the old North Shore had died at Carpiquet. When the 189 casualties from June are added to the Carpiquet losses, the figure from June 6 to July 9 comes to 478 killed, wounded, and missing, the equivalent of the rifle strength of the battalion. The replacements came from the general army pool and included officers, NCOs and men from across Canada. It is true that the NSR would never again be that tight band of rugged northern New Brunswickers. But the battalion had made the best of an impossible task on D-Day and at Carpiquet won an unheralded victory against the odds, with its spirit and cadre intact, an achievement that some in the army noticed. In any event, the campaign in northwest Europe was just getting started: there was still work to be done.

The Day A Robin Sang at Carpiquet
by R.F. Foran

The following poem has been a part of my psyche since that day in 1944, it would be July 6, 7, or 8. I am not sure of the exact date at this juncture, we went in on the attack on July 4 to secure the airfield and surrounding area.

In all of human conflict, in wars, great and small, in battles honored by history or never mentioned in any of the annals of war, there are, I am sure, to each and every combatant, their own private war, their own supreme test of courage and endurance.

To me, Carpiquet represented my war, although when measured against the grand scale of battles in North Africa, Russia, the Pacific, etc. it scarcely deserves a mention. To me however it was really my World War 2.

However this poem is not really about this battle, fierce as it may have been. This poem is about a strange awakening to the fact that after almost four years of preparing for the inevitability of war and all that it entailed, there is the sudden shock of knowing that we can dare hope again for peace, and home, and love, and family, and all the things that war denies.

After days of constant artillery bombardment which saw the stately trees in our hedgerow totally denuded of leaves until their gaunt limbs pointed an accusing finger Heavenward and as if to say God, how can you allow your creatures to treat each other in this manner. After watching a number of green replacements arrive, so close to an enemy attack that they would have little or no chance to dig in and therefore survive the terrible night, it seemed so incongruous that when the battle had finally ended and the bloated and rotting corpses of the enemy littered the field in front of our lines that the sun would rise to vaporize a morning dew and that on a small bush I would see a robin sing his song of hope, of renewal, in the face of all this carnage. Suddenly hope is born anew. This war is only a crazy farce, real people will re-build a new and better world, my homesickness would be only a memory, an illusion of something which had never really happened.

'Comrades gather around me'
In this morning's sweet still air
You from Baie du Vin or Miramichi
Listen to this song so sweet and clear.

This robin has survived, a nest to build
Forget the smell of cordite, death and all
Remember that we too can dare to hope
Midst sound of war, Peace gives her siren call.

Perhaps like me, a son of Restigouche
This strife has merely postponed love's sweet hour
And like our red-breasted friend in yonder bush
Hope like seeds will one day burst in flower.

Standing here, so humbled by this song
I dare not say, and you will agree
How many from this brave New Brunswick throng
Will live to taste the fruits of victory.
However, for this moment, frozen in time
Listening to his song with hope so gay
Let me thank my Maker for this hour
The day a robin sang at Carpiquet.

— *G22244 Sgt. R.F. Foran*
Carpiquet, France, July 8, 1944

Photo Credits

Photos and other illustrative material on the front and back covers appear courtesy of the Canadian War Museum (CWM); on page 6 and odd-numbered pages courtesy of the Canadian Forces Film Unit; on pages 8, 28, 46, 76, 78, 84, 104, and 110 courtesy of Library and Archives Canada (LAC); on page 18 courtesy of Ken Wetherby; on pages 22, 60, 63, and 96 courtesy of 2nd Battalion The Royal New Brunswick Regiment (2RNBR); on page 24 courtesy of the Carleton County Historical Society; on page 25 courtesy of Fred Moar; on pages 30 and 88 courtesy of Mike Bechthold; on pages 34, 38, and 40 courtesy of the New Brunswick Museum (NBM); on pages 42, 70, and 92 courtesy of the Laurier Centre for Military, Strategic and Disarmament Studies (LCMSDS); on page 48 courtesy of the Ville de St. Aubin; on pages 50, 56, and 106 courtesy of the Imperial War Museum (IWM); on page 64 courtesy of M. Cassigneul; on page 108 courtesy of the Ville de Carpiquet; and on pages 116 and 118 courtesy of Matt Symes.

Selected Bibliography

The regimental history, *The North Shore (New Brunswick) Regiment* by Will R. Bird (Fredericton: University Press, 1963), remains the only comprehensive history of the unit and provides a gold mine of first-person accounts of actions. Myles Hickey's marvellous account of his time as the regiment's padre, *The Scarlet Dawn* (Campbellton, NB: Tribune Publishers, 1949), is a classic in the literature on the Canadian experience in the Second World War. C.P. Stacey's official army history volume, *The Victory Campaign* (Ottawa: Queen's Printer, 1960), provides the essential context for the NSR story. It should be read in conjunction with Terry Copp's recent *Fields of Fire: The Canadians in Normandy* (Toronto: University of Toronto Press, 2003) in order to obtain a more modern view of events. Most accounts of the D-Day landings say little about the North Shore; most quote simply from Hickey. None attempts to follow the regiment's efforts systematically, except Tim Saunders' recent guidebook, *Juno Beach* (Barnsley, UK: Pen and Sword Books, 2003). No modern scholarship exists on the Carpiquet battle. It was dismissed as a failure at the time and the interpretation has remained ossified ever since. Both Stacey and Copp discuss Carpiquet, focusing on the failure to take the southern hangers and the airport control buildings. For some inexplicable reason, historians have not looked closely at the NSR experience and its key role in stopping the German counter-attacks and destroying their operational reserve in the Caen sector.

For a virtual tour of the sites described in this book see: www.unb.ca/nbmhp/05_books.htm

Acknowledgements

All projects of this type owe an enormous debt to a great many people and this one is no exception. Terry Copp and his staff at the Wilfrid Laurier Centre for Military, Strategic and Disarmament Studies encouraged the work from the outset and provided an initial burst of documents and crucial aerial photos. Lieutenant-Colonel Greg MacCallum and the headquarters of 2 RNBR in Bathurst helped with other sources, as did Graham Wiseman of the North Shore Regimental Association. The Canadian Battlefield Foundation allowed me to shape the 2006 Normandy Study Tour to help sort out the story, and its Vice President (France), Celine Garbay, did much of the essential work in France, contacting mayors and securing information and illustrations. Study Tour participants Alex Carrette, Chuck Gruchy, Nic Clarke, and Matt Symes walked with me through the D-Day landings with map, aerial photos, and war diary to work things out, and Celine kindly arranged access to the château grounds at Tailleville. Allain Cormier of the Provincial Archives of NB put me in touch with Arnaud Blin, a French film producer, and Arnaud and Xavier Paturel of the Juno Beach Centre secured some remarkable information and material from la ville de St. Aubin-sur-Mer. I am grateful to Mr. Cassigneul, the mayor of Tailleville, for his help. Brandon Savage arranged an interview with his grandfather, Bill Savage, the only survivor from the ambush of A Company HQ on D-Day. North Shore veterans Fenton Daley, Warren Steen, and especially Fred Moar also endured interviews — in Fred's case repeatedly. Special thanks to Kim Anderson for allowing me to use the papers of Brigadier J.E. Anderson, and Ron Cormier for sharing his insights.

I am grateful to the following for providing illustrations for the book: the Canadian War Museum, Library and Archives of Canada, Canadian

Forces Photo Unit, CFB Gagetown Museum, the New Brunswick Museum, la ville de St. Aubin-sur-Mer, la ville de Carpiquet, Major Tim Saunders, the Imperial War Museum, Ken Weatherby, Matt Symes, Fred Moar, and Kevin Norris. Rob Blanchard and Matt Wiley from UNB helped with photos. Mike Bechthold did his usual great job on maps, while Deb Stapleford kindly did the final editorial corrections. Many people endured my persistent preaching about the neglected story the book tells, and I am grateful for their forbearance. Brent Wilson — the son of a Queen's Own D-Day vet — suffered the worst in this, and did a superb job editing the book. Julie Scriver and Angela Williams of Goose Lane Editions did their usual outstanding job of design and editing. I am especially grateful to Mrs. Betty Murray, daughter of the late Will R. Bird, for her kind permission to quote from her father's history of the North Shore Regiment. Finally, thanks to Bobbi for enduring the distractions and grumpiness of another book project.

Index

The New Brunswick Military History Museum

The mission of the New Brunswick Military History Museum is to collect, preserve, research, and exhibit artifacts which illustrate the history and heritage of the military forces in New Brunswick and New Brunswickers at war, during peacetime, and on United Nations or North Atlantic Treaty Organization duty.

The New Brunswick Military History Museum is proud to partner with the Gregg Centre.
Highlighting 400 years of New Brunswick's history.

www.nbmilitaryhistorymuseum.ca
www.museehistoiremilitairenb.ca
info@nbmilitaryhistorymuseum.ca

The New Brunswick Military Heritage Project

The New Brunswick Military Heritage Project, a non-profit organization devoted to public awareness of the remarkable military heritage of the province, is an initiative of the Brigadier Milton F. Gregg, VC, Centre for the Study of War and Society of the University of New Brunswick. The organization consists of museum professionals, teachers, university professors, graduate students, active and retired members of the Canadian Forces, and other historians. We welcome public involvement. People who have ideas for books or information for our database can contact us through our Web site: www.unb.ca/nbmhp.

One of the main activities of the New Brunswick Military Heritage Project is the publication of the New Brunswick Military Heritage Series with Goose Lane Editions. This series of books is under the direction of Marc Milner, Director of the Gregg Centre, and J. Brent Wilson, Research Director of the Gregg Centre at the University of New Brunswick. Publication of the series is supported by a grant from the Canadian War Musuem.

The New Brunswick Military Heritage Series

Volume 1 *Saint John Fortifications, 1630-1956*,
Roger Sarty and Doug Knight

Volume 2 *Hope Restored: The American Revolution and the
Founding of New Brunswick*, Robert L. Dallison

Volume 3 *The Siege of Fort Beauséjour, 1755*, Chris M. Hand

Volume 4 *Riding into War: The Memoir of a Horse Transport Driver,
1916-1919*, James Robert Johnston

Volume 5 *The Road to Canada: The Grand Communications Route
from Saint John to Quebec*, W.E. (Gary) Campbell

Volume 6 *Trimming Yankee Sails: Pirates and Privateers
of New Brunswick*, Faye Kert

Volume 7 *War on the Home Front: The Farm Diaries of Daniel MacMillan,
1914-1927*, ed. Bill Parenteau and Stephen Dutcher

Volume 8 *Turning Back the Fenians: New Brunswick's
Last Colonial Campaign*, Robert L. Dallison

Volume 9 *D-Day to Carpiquet: The North Shore Regiment
and the Liberation of Europe*, Marc Milner

About the Author

Marc Milner, a native of Sackville, NB, attended the University of New Brunswick where he earned a BA in 1977, an MA in 1979, and his Doctorate in 1983. His dissertation was published by University of Toronto Press in 1985 as *North Atlantic Run: The Royal Canadian Navy and the Battle for the Convoys*. From 1983 to 1986, Milner was an historian with the Directorate of History, Department of National Defence, Ottawa. While there, he wrote portions of volume II of the RCAF's official *History* dealing with maritime air operations and the first narrative of the new official history of the Royal Canadian Navy. Milner joined the History Department at UNB in 1986 and from then until 2005 was Director of UNB's Military and Strategic Studies Program. Among his other chores, he was formerly Chairman of the Canadian Military Colleges Advisory Board; he served as an editor for the journal, *Canadian Military History*; and has conducted student study tours of battlefields in Europe on behalf of the Canadian Battlefields Foundation, of which he is a member of the Board of Directors, and the Canadian Armed Forces. He is currently the Vice-Chair of the Board of Visitors of the Canadian Forces College, Chair of the UNB History Department, and Director of UNB's Brigadier Milton F. Gregg, VC, Centre for the Study of War and Society.

Milner is best known for his work on Canadian naval history. Since the appearance of his first major book in 1985, he has published *The U-Boat Hunters: The Royal Canadian Navy and the Offensive against Germany's Submarines* (1995); *Corvettes of the Royal Canadian Navy* (co-authored with Ken Macpherson in 1993); a novel, *Incident at North Point* (1998); a popular history, *HMCS Sackville 1940-1985* (1998) for the Canadian Naval Memorial Trust; and *Canada's Navy: The First*

Century (1999). He has also edited *Canadian Military History: Selected Readings* (1993); and co-edited *Military History and the Military Profession* (1992). His articles have appeared in *Military Affairs, Acadiensis, RCN in Retrospect, Canadian Defence Quarterly, Horizon Canada, The RUSI Journal, Journal of Strategic Studies, The New Canadian Encyclopaedia, The Oxford Companion to the Second World War* and elsewhere. He is co-director of the New Brunswick Military Heritage Project and writes a regular column on naval history for *Legion Magazine*. His latest work, *Battle of the Atlantic*, was published by Tempus Publishing, UK, in 2003, and was awarded the Charles P. Stacey Prize for the best book on military history in Canada for 2003-2004.